MATCHROOM SNOOKER

STEVE DAVIS

JIMMY WHITE · DENNIS TAYLOR · NEAL FOULDS
WILLIE THORNE · TERRY GRIFFITHS · TONY MEO

Introduction
BY
BARRY HEARN

PELHAM BOOKS

Matchroom Snooker was planned and written by Julian Worthington in conjunction with the Matchroom players. All the photographs were especially taken for the book by Terry Trott with the exception of the frontispiece photograph by Richard McLaren Photography and the photograph on page 149 by Eric Whitehead Photography. All the diagrams were prepared by Guy Smith. The book was designed by Tim McPhee and produced by Debbie Wright, both of Book Production Consultants, 47 Norfolk Street, Cambridge.

PELHAM BOOKS

Published by the Penguin Group
27 Wrights Lane, London W8 5TZ, England
Viking Penguin Inc., 40 West 23rd Street, New York, New York 10010, USA
Penguin Books Australia Ltd, Ringwood, Victoria, Australia
Penguin Books Canada Ltd, 2801 John Street, Markham, Ontario, Canada L3R 1B4
Penguin Books (NZ) Ltd, 182–190 Wairau Road, Auckland 10, New Zealand

Penguin Books Ltd, Registered Offices: Harmondsworth, Middlesex, England

First published 1988

British Library Cataloguing in Publication Data

Davis, Steve, *1957 –*
    Matchroom snooker.
    1. Snooker-Manuals
    I. Title
    974.7'35

ISBN 0 7207 1826 0

Typeset in Times Roman by Cambridge Photosetting Services, Cambridge

Origination by Anglia Graphics Ltd, Bedford

Printed in Great Britain by Butler and Tanner Ltd, Frome and London

CONTENTS

INTRODUCTION

BY BARRY HEARN

Matchroom was really born in March 1976, when I first met Steve Davis. Its achievements to date naturally reflect Steve's development as a player and his charisma as a person. This is one of the great strengths of Matchroom and, I am sure, this book too. As the world's number one, he acts very much as a pillar for the team and has extended this role to introduce you to the other members, their style and technique in the pages that follow.

As with the Matchroom motto, this book illustrates and, I hope, will teach you the 'pursuit of excellence' on the snooker table. It is certainly my belief that as the Matchroom players have proved to be the best in the world on the table, so they will inspire others through this book to follow in their footsteps.

While writing this Introduction, I am delighted to be able to announce the addition of Cliff Thorburn to the Matchroom team. Cliff epitomises all the qualities of the true professional and I know will enhance the reputation of the game both on and off the table, which is very much part of the Matchroom policy.

The main reason why I feel *Matchroom Snooker* will be of genuine interest to everyone is because of the variety offered through the personalities involved. In Matchroom we have every type of person, which I regard as very important since the way you play snooker is reflected in your own personality. It is an extension of that individual personality. Someone, for example, who lives his life 'in the fast lane' will play his snooker that way. The steadier, more calculated person will approach the game in that context.

The Matchroom players reflect every age group and aspect of life and this is extended to their approach on the table – from Jimmy White and Tony Meo at one end of the spectrum to Dennis Taylor and Terry Griffiths at the other. That is the inherent strength of Matchroom and, I believe, this book as well.

It is a fact of life that there are no hard and fast rules when it comes to playing snooker. No one can say: "You must do it exactly like this." Every player, at whatever level, must develop his or her game within their own characteristics.

In *Matchroom Snooker* each player reflects his own personal view on how he approaches the game. No two players will necessarily agree with each other on particular aspects – nor should they. If they did, there would be no discussion – and no book of this nature.

At this point it is very important to stress that you should not attempt just to absorb the information and follow it religiously. My advice is to read the book and learn what you can from it, but at the same time try to interpret what it says within your own personality and characteristics. This not only includes your physical build and capability but also your mental approach.

I hope all who read *Matchroom Snooker* will be able to identify those parts of their own personality that fit in with individual players. If you can highlight those aspects that suit you and your style, you will find that adopting them is a natural and automatic consequence.

If you feel that your personality is more in line with that of Steve, you will tend to adopt those aspects of his play that suit yours, too. If you are of a similar temperament to Willie Thorne and enjoy concentrating on building high breaks, then you will probably try to adapt to his style of play. Equally, if you tend to take a purist's attitude and enjoy analysing your technique, then you will necessarily concentrate on what Terry Griffiths has to say.

WHAT IS MATCHROOM?

As I built the Matchroom team, the most important credential was that all the players were friends and mixed well together. Of course, they had to be winners, too, since the concept of Matchroom is all about winning. And the success of the team, both on and off the table, is a direct consequence of both elements.

Allied to this, naturally, is the development and demonstration of professionalism in its purist sense. This, I believe, is an essential characteristic that must run through any player who is serious about achievement. It is the responsibility of any sport to reflect this professionalism, not just for the image of the game but also as an inspiration to young players.

Naturally Matchroom has strong commercial undertones as well, which inevitably follow when a sport is upgraded in the way snooker has been in recent years. This is clearly illustrated by the fact that from small clubs and smoke-filled back street halls, snooker is now the number one television viewing sport.

But its maturity and appeal stretch way beyond the small screen. Probably for the first time since we showed the world how to play football, we are now successfully exporting our own game across the world to countries that had never seen it before.

I am naturally proud and delighted that it is the Matchroom professionals who are leading the way in the development of the sport overseas, giving the benefit of their skills to millions of people the world over.

THE MATCHROOM TEAM

As I have already said, each member of the Matchroom team is an individual, with his own personality, talent and characteristics.

When one talks about Steve, one immediately associates him with professionalism, application and the pursuit of perfection. He is the type of player who can readily adjust to changing circumstances on the table. He has that extra element of granite-like determination – the dead-eye look – which separates winners from just triers. I feel Steve is very much in the mould of the modern-day American sportsman, who is totally dedicated, totally professional and must win to justify these qualities.

At the other end of the scale you have Jimmy White, probably the most popular of current players and the hero of present-day snooker. He plays completely from instinct, improvises virtually every shot and has that indefinable quality you cannot pick up from the pages of a book. Because the risk factor in his game is so high, however, he doesn't win as much as he could. But for sheer entertainment value there is none better.

In many ways Neal Foulds is the epitome of the new breed of snooker player –the fully dedicated professional in the Davis mould with that killer instinct and will to get to the top. For many this involves hour upon hour of serious practice, in stark contrast to the flair players, for whom practice is not such a critical aspect of the game. In Neal we see the new professional, whose approach includes thorough preparation for every match.

Terry Griffiths epitomises a totally different type of player – one who had a very strong amateur involvement for a number of years and, by today's standards, joined the professional ranks comparatively late in his playing career.

This as much as anything would help explain his acute awareness for the need of thorough groundwork and a very large emphasis on technique. He therefore spends much more time than the average players on analysing his own game, right from the basics of cue action, and looking for ways to improve his own very high standards.

In contrast to those who seem to accept when they have reached a certain level and only look to improve their tactical awareness, Terry concentrates on the physical aspects of the game – more than any of the Matchroom players, even Steve himself.

Dennis Taylor is another of the traditional style players, who remembers well the days when there was little work around. He therefore makes the most of every opportunity and has developed an invaluable characteristic – that of a fighter. Although he doesn't have the flamboyancy of a Jimmy White or the dedication to practice of a Neal Foulds, he does have the brain and experience and the gift of remembering virtually every shot. All these qualities have made him a much harder player – probably the hardest of the Matchroom team.

I regard Willie Thorne as a player who bridges the gap between the old and new schools. He too had a successful amateur career and was one of the youngest players of the time to turn professional. For anyone wanting to master the art of break-building, Willie is obviously the one to follow. His reputation as Mr Maximum has come from his expertise around the pink and black spots, the one area of the table he has concentrated on in practice over the last 15 years.

Another specialist around the pink and black spots is Tony Meo, a player much in the style of Jimmy. Tony was in fact the youngest player at the time to make a maximum break. In contrast to players like Steve, Terry or Dennis, who use more safety play to create openings, Tony will attack the balls and take on potting chances to set up opportunities for a break. He is a gritty player whose skills more than make up for his size.

So that, in essence, is the Matchroom team – one of individuals with different characters and different skills. Their strengths are more reflective of their own personalities than any positive indication of the best approach to the game from a technical or mental point of view. And at any level, particularly in the top professional game, the way any situation is read is very much down to the individual, the pattern of play and how each player sees the percentages in any given shot. It is up to you to decide what type of player you really are and to use those aspects of the Matchroom players' methods and approach that you feel suit you best.

USING THE BOOK

What *Matchroom Snooker* should tell you is that, once you have mastered the basic techniques, there is no right or wrong way of playing the game. When you are at the table, only you can decide how to tackle the situation that confronts you.

So what is the best way to use the book? If you are a born snooker player – a natural – you will read the book and I am sure find it interesting. But I doubt you will want to learn much from it. But here I am talking probably about one in a million!

For us mortals *Matchroom Snooker* should provide an invaluable reference book, one that you should read step-by-step and then go back to it as often as necessary to master those skills essential for a successful competitive player. Its benefit should be that of a coach, providing a constant reminder and check as you progress through all the techniques.

Snooker is a game of techniques and *Matchroom Snooker* is a technical book. As such it should be used more like a can of oil. You will need to lubricate all parts of your game at regular intervals to keep moving – and in the right direction.

EQUIPMENT

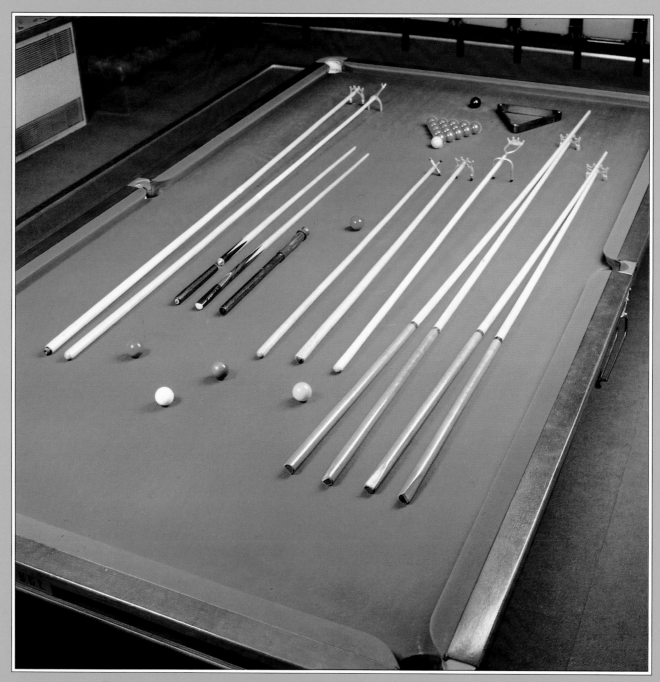

The range of equipment that has been designed for use on the snooker table is very comprehensive. The main items shown here (from left) are the long spider, the long swan neck, two-piece and one-piece cues, a slot-on extension, the standard rest, the spider, the extended spider and the long rests with half-butts.

INTRODUCTION
BY STEVE DAVIS

In this first section of the book, Tony explains about the equipment used to play snooker and stresses the importance of having a cue that suits you and how to look after it properly.

The most significant change recently has been the cue extension, which has really made the half-butt obsolete, particularly in the professional game. It is strange to think that for some time this piece of equipment has been used by people playing in wheel-chairs, but only in the last few years has it become a standard item for the professional players.

One of the earliest types, which Cliff Thorburn started using, was an extension that fitted in the middle of his two-piece cue. The problem with it was that it took so long to fit together and then remove. It is important to have an extension that you can fix on easily and quickly to prevent upsetting your rhythm between shots.

There have been other types of cue made, such as the extended – or telescopic – version and also cues with tips you don't have to chalk. Another variation was the five-piece cue, which was very compact and would fit into a small briefcase. One manufacturer even made a cue within a walking stick. Unfortunately the butt had to be hollow, which made the cue too light. Other hollow cues have been produced in aluminium to prevent warping. The only problem here is that if you lent on them they would bend and you couldn't straighten them properly. Carbon fibre is another material being experimented with at the moment.

The trouble with all such innovations is that good players cannot afford to try them out for too long in case they do not work. It takes a lot of courage to change your cue and most professsionals would much rather play with the one they were used to. That is what makes the cue so valuable – regardless of what it is and how much it cost.

EQUIPMENT

BY TONY MEO

If you are serious about learning to play snooker as well as possible – or feel that by working harder at your game you can become a better player, then the first place to start is with your cue. Personally I don't believe the choice is simply between a good or a bad cue. At the end of the day it is basically a question of individual preference.

The cue is, of course, the single most important piece of equipment and acts as an extension to your arm. It must therefore suit you and feel right – in your hand, through your bridge and on the rest.

You do not have to spend a fortune on a cue. Believe it or not, I bought mine secondhand for just £3! Obviously it has to be as straight as possible, although you are unlikely to find one that is perfectly straight. As a general rule, do not go for extremes – too light or too heavy, too thin or too thick.

Cues are normally made from ash or maple, the main difference between these being in the grain. With ash, the grain is far more prominent. Some players, such as Steve, prefer this type since they recognise the line of the grain and this ensures that they always hold the cue in the same way.

The main advantage of this is that eventually most cues will develop a slight warp and by using your cue in the same way every time you automatically compensate for this. Also, your eye gets used to a particular line down the cue and you are then less likely to be distracted when playing a shot.

The standard cue is 4 ft 10 in. long and the average weight is around 17 oz. These measurements obviously vary from player to player. Steve, for example, plays with a 4 ft 9¼ in. cue which weighs 18¾ oz. I personally like a lighter cue (mine weighs about 17½ oz), which I find suits my game since I regard myself as a touch player. But the final decision is yours as to whether you prefer your cue to be on the heavier or lighter side.

People talk about the balance of a cue, but this is difficult to advise on because again what may feel right for me would not necessarily suit someone else. You need to have a reasonable amount of weight in the butt end and the cue must feel firm and solid in the hand when playing a shot. But it should not be top heavy and the butt should always fit comfortably in the hand – not too large and not too small.

Although I play with a one-piece cue, certainly the two-piece is much more convenient and nowadays is up to top standard. Initially the joints were prone to wear, but this problem has generally been overcome and there is really no difference in quality between the two types.

The advantages of the two-piece cue are obvious. You can pack it away in a smaller case, which is much more convenient to carry around. Equally, you can change the shaft on a two-piece, something that Cliff Thorburn does, incidentally. Jimmy and Steve have a specially adapted threequarter two-piece cue with a screw-on butt end that will also take an extension. I will talk about extensions in a minute.

Make sure when you look for a cue that it has a ferrule fitted at the tip end. This is most important because the metal or fibre ring not only helps prevent the end of the cue from splitting but also protects it from possible damage when you are fitting and shaping the tip.

Although, as I said earlier, it is difficult to advise on exactly what type of cue to buy, I would certainly recommend that you go for a two-piece cue. It should definitely play as well and is a lot more convenient.

Depending on how much you want to pay, there is little doubt in my mind that older cues which were handmade involved much better workmanship. You can tell these by the rounded splicing at the butt end. Modern machined cues have a pyramid-shaped splice. But the hand-made cues are more expensive.

CUE EXTENSIONS

The cue extension, which has only recently been introduced, is a marvellous invention because it saves you having to use the half-butt, a clumsy and unwieldy piece of equipment.

With the half-butt, which just feels like a long piece of wood with a tip on the end, trying to pot a ball was just guesswork and has often cost players a frame – and sometimes the match. I could never understand why it took so long for this very useful piece of equipment to be developed.

The great advantage of the extension is that it is part of your own cue and, of course, you are using your own cue tip. It is also rigid and allows you to do virtually anything you want with the cue ball, as you would with the basic cue. Not only can you pot with much greater confidence, but you can also screw back or use side, something you would never dare attempt with the half-butt.

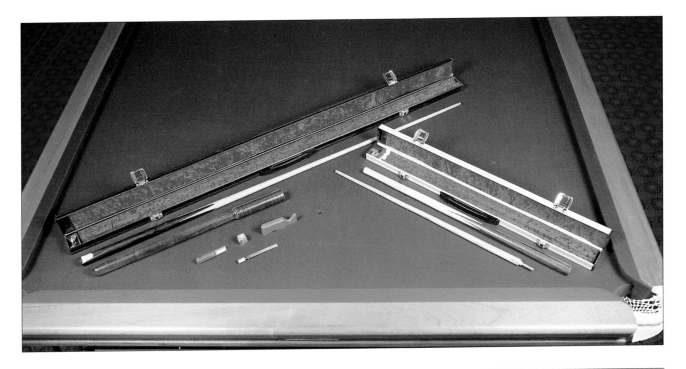

You have the choice of a one-piece or two-piece cue. The latter is more convenient and enables you to use a screw-on extension. There is also a range of accessories, including (from left) cue tip shapers, chalk, files and a rest support for use on the cushion.

The best type of extension is the one that screws in, which obviously can only be used with two-piece cues. This helps you retain a really solid feel of the cue. With my one-piece cue, I use an extension that is threaded inside. As you turn it, so it clamps around the butt of the cue.

This feels and works much better than the ordinary extensions which have either a plastic or rubber joint that locks on to the end of the cue. These do have a tendency to wobble a bit and are not so rigid. For beginners, they are certainly a great improvement on the half-butt. For someone who is well into their game, however, the screw-in type is definitely the best.

With the extension, there is really no excuse now for missing a shot, as long as you are used to handling a longer cue. So it is important to practise with it for those occasions when you cannot reach with your own cue.

CUE TIP

The condition of the tip of your cue is absolutely critical since it is this that makes contact with the cue ball. Although every player has his own preference for the exact state of the tip, it should not be too hard or too soft. If it is too hard, you will not achieve any grip on the ball. If it is too soft, it will compress too much on contact and certain types of shot, particularly when you are using side, will be virtually impossible.

Most players prefer a dome-shaped tip, although some like it to be virtually flat, while others keep the tip rounded, more like a football. My tip is always semi-domed, while Steve uses one that looks more like a mushroom! In contrast, Dennis keeps his a bit squarer.

You can shape the tip by using a file. Be careful not to damage the tip and always file downwards to prevent lifting it off the end of the cue. When it is new, the tip is soft and rounded and will need a lot of playing in before it hardens up and gives you a consistent contact with the cue ball. For this reason we would always file a new tip down to the desired shape. With regular tournaments, the professional does not have time to play a new tip in.

After a while the surface of the tip will become hard, smooth and shiny with use and will not hold the chalk, which tends to cake on the top. In this case you can rough up the surface slightly by tapping it with your file.

One trick I have learnt is to lick my finger and moisten the top of the tip. This helps to soften it enough to take the chalk. By this stage, your tip is on the way out, but it does help to keep it going until you are in a position to change it.

Left: The shape of the cue tip varies between players, although most including myself prefer it to be semi-domed.
Above: When using a file to shape your cue tip, always work with downward strokes to prevent lifting the tip and be careful

not to damage the end of the cue.
Right: You can also use the file to compress a tip if it is too soft and, by tapping the top gently, rough up the surface slightly if it becomes caked with chalk.

CHALK

It is very important to keep the tip of your cue properly chalked, since this helps improve the grip on the cue ball. This is particularly so when you are trying to spin the ball – either using side or screwing the shot.

You will notice how we always chalk our tips before every shot. This is a good habit to get into, although you must not overdo the chalk so that it is caked on. Just wipe it gently a couple of times over the tip – and never grind it on.

Most professionals use green chalk, since it does not seem to mark the cue ball so noticeably as the more common blue chalk. Avoid cheaper chalks,

since these are much harder and will not come off on the tip as easily.

CUE CASE

After your cue, this is probably the most important item since, having got the cue you like and play best with, you must make sure you protect it. The type of case will naturally depend on whether you have a one or two-piece cue. But it must be solid and hold the cue firmly. The inside should be well padded to give the cue maximum protection and prevent it from moving about.

Most players carry around a trouble-shooting kit in their case for emergency repairs. This normally includes spare tips (new or worn), a knife, sandpaper, glue, a file, etc.

Of course you do not just have to look after your

cue in the case. There are several golden rules to follow when you are using it.

LOOKING AFTER THE CUE

You must never lean your cue up against a wall for any length of time, since the extra pressure could cause it to warp. Equally you must keep it away from direct heat, such as a fire or radiator, or in a particularly warm environment such as a car in hot weather. If it is subjected to high temperatures, the wood will dry out and make the cue quite brittle. In extreme circumstances it could even break if dropped.

The cue will, of course, get dirty with use and will need to be cleaned regularly. I use a damp cloth to rub it up and down, which takes off all the excess dirt and leaves the cue nice and smooth. Don't be tempted to use sandpaper on it, since that will take some of the wood away.

Every six months or so I oil my cue. For this I use linseed oil, which helps prevent the wood going brittle.

A smooth cue is obviously very important. I noticed when playing in Canada that a lot of people used to chalk their hands or sprinkle talcum powder over them when playing in very warm conditions to ensure the cue moved smoothly. This does tend to be rather messy, but it certainly has the desired effect.

THE TABLE

One of the basic problems with snooker tables is that each one will play differently. Either this is because of the table itself or the conditions around it. The only way to master a table is to make sure that you play on as many different ones as possible and make a mental note as to how they react in different ways.

The main factors that effect the way a table plays include the overall temperature, humidity, the condition of the cloth and the wear on the cushions. Without getting too technical at this stage, one of the most important aspects of the table is the nap of the cloth.

A new cloth should have plenty of nap, which is basically its texture. Tables are brushed with the nap, that is from the baulk (or break-off) end to the top of the table. So striking the ball up the table you are playing with the nap. From the top end towards baulk you are playing against the nap. Incidentally, the ball travels slightly faster with the nap than against it. The other effects are discussed later in the book.

With a new table, or one that has recently been reclothed, you will find there is plenty of nap. With an old table, the nap will be worn and will therefore have little effect.

There are many different grades of cloth. The richer the green, the more nap there is – which certainly tends to help those shots with side but equally can cause the ball to roll off line. As the cloth wears, the colour turns to a lighter green and in places may even appear to shine. This means it is getting right down to the slate bed and balls will roll much faster across it. Control therefore tends to be a lot more difficult.

If you get the chance, it is well worth testing out a table that you are not used to. There are several exercises you can do to see how that table is playing.

One of these is to roll the white ball from the pink spot gently towards the middle pockets to check how it runs. You will find that you often have to pot into these pockets and you can test the cloth for any idiosyncrasies.

A snooker table set up for the break-off. The standard size table is 12ft by 6ft. Although pocket sizes are being standardised, you will still find variations between tables. And, of course, more importantly every table has its own characteristics and will play slightly differently.

A similar test is to put the cue ball on the black spot and gently roll it towards the top pockets. Check to see whether it pulls at all or goes straight in. Again, when you have learnt to build up your game, you should find yourself using these pockets a lot.

Because of the importance of the top cushion, since that is where most of the reds and of course the black ball often need to be played off, you should check this as well. Roll the cue ball along this top cushion to see whether it hugs it or not. To have control over this end of the table can be crucial in winning or losing a frame.

To check the length of the table you should roll the cue ball up and down to see whether it runs off at all. If there is any natural deviation, you can make allowances for this when going for specific shots. Although this may sound ultra-meticulous, it can make the difference between getting or losing a pot – and possibly the frame as well.

Testing the cushions is not that easy. Normally you learn to adjust to them as you play. Certainly a professional would expect to have mastered the table within a couple of frames. With amateurs, one would expect to take longer. This is the major problem of playing on different tables. Through practice you can get used to one table and then find you have to play a match on another which is completely strange to you. But that is part of the game of snooker and one you must master to become a successful player.

When it comes to potting, the pockets are, of course, all important. Some tables have tight pockets, others have easy ones. But when we talk of this, we are not referring to the size of the opening, but the way in which the pockets are cut.

I have played on tables with what we call buckets, where you could fit two balls into each pocket. But if they are not well cut, they offer no advantage with the pot. A lot of people think that it is the size of the pockets that makes the difference between a ball going in and staying out. But that simply is not true.

You can test this by throwing a ball down the cushion towards a pocket. Depending on how the pocket is cut, the ball can either bobble about or go straight in. If a table has well undercut pockets, potting is a lot easier.

The other aspect of a strange table is the pace across the cloth. You can test this by rolling a ball hard, up and down, and seeing how many lengths of

the table it travels. On average it should run at least five lengths of the table. On a fast table this could be six – or four on a slow table.

Although the condition of the table is only relevant once you have mastered the basic techniques, it is important to be able to 'test' a strange one before you play on it. Because, however well you play your shots, the way that table is playing can make all the difference to your game.

THE BALLS

There is a lot of difference between the snooker of old and that of the present day, particularly in the type of balls used. Originally these were of ivory, which was much heavier, and therefore touch play was far more difficult. Over the years the balls have got lighter, which makes it a great deal easier to effect spin and to control the movement.

The ones used now – Super Crystalate – offer the player far greater scope in what can be done and the type of shots that can be played. Equally, they are less demanding on the cue tip, since with heavier balls you had to strike much harder. This meant that timing of the shot was more critical as well.

PRACTICE
TESTING THE TABLE

To test the pace of a strange table and the spring in the cushions, throw a ball up as hard as you can and see how many times it runs up and down. On average it should cover about five lengths of the table, but could vary between four and six.

To check on how the pockets are cut, roll a ball fairly hard into each in turn, particularly along the cushions, and see how easily the jaws accept it.

Another exercise I use which helps you to gauge how the top end of the table plays is to put the cue ball on the pink spot and roll it gently into both centre pockets in turn. Then use a similar exercise with the cue ball on the black spot, rolling it into the two top pockets. Then roll the black along the top cushion in each direction and see how well it hugs the cushion. On a good table, in each case the ball should roll straight in.

BASIC SNOOKER

INTRODUCTION
BY STEVE DAVIS

Terry Griffiths joined the Matchroom after a tremendous spell of snooker during 1979 and 1980, during which time he seemed to win just about everything in sight, including of course the world championship in his first season as a professional. Anyone who knows or has met Terry cannot but be impressed by his honesty and integrity. He also has a great sense of humour, which does not necessarily come across on the television.

One aspect I have always respected him for is the time he devotes to the amateur game. Of all the current professional players, he probably does more in the way of coaching and showing others how to play the game than anyone I know. In general, most top players prefer to play than teach. Terry loves to play but he also gets tremendous satisfaction from watching others and helping them develop their techniques.

I am sure there is a benefit in this approach, since by going back and analysing the basics – how to stand, how to hold the cue, how to develop a good cueing action, etc – you never lose sight of the most important part of snooker, those elementary techniques without which you can never master the sport.

Terry is one of the most conscientious of players when it comes to technique. He is constantly checking on why things are going wrong – or right. He is not satisfied just to play the game for the sake of it and accept that he will go through good and bad patches, as we all do. He wants to know why he's having a good spell – or a bad one. In this respect he is the best example for anyone learning the game or wanting to improve it, since if you can look closely at yourself and how you are playing, you may well spend a lot less time playing badly.

Obviously in any sport, if you haven't got the very basic techniques right, you will never give your natural ability a real chance to flourish. In this section Terry Griffiths analyses the basic techniques required to build up your game and stresses how important it is to master these before you can hope to develop the more advanced skills required for successful competitive snooker.

There are, of course, variations in technique from player to player, whether at a basic or more advanced level. But it is vitally important that you concentrate on establishing a sound and simple technique at this basic level. As you become more familiar with the game, you will find you can stamp your own identity on it. But take it from me that if at any time you start to stray from these basic techniques you will soon find yourself in trouble.

Travelling around the clubs, I see a lot of keen amateur players who either do not know about or who have ignored these basic principles. I've watched people cue over their knuckles, between the index and middle fingers, because they haven't gone to the trouble of developing a proper bridge. Some hold the cue with their thumb on the top of it. Their argument is that it feels more comfortable that way. I have pointed out that unless they are prepared to change these, they will never progress beyond a certain standard in the game.

I have seen these same players some time later and they are still playing that way. When I challenge them, they tell me that they did try the other way but they didn't play very well and so they went back to their old style.

I mention this because it highlights the enormous problem of starting again – from scratch. It is a very brave thing to do to make yourself play worse to get better. But that is the discipline you must follow if you want to improve the standard of your game. And this is what Terry is doing in this section. It is quite likely that most of you reading this book have played before. But you must have the courage to forget what you have learnt in the past and be prepared to start again. By following the basic techniques that Terry describes, I am sure you will quickly discover those areas where you are going wrong. Be prepared to work hard to get them right. After a while you will be amazed at the difference it will make to your overall game if you do.

PREPARING TO PLAY

BY TERRY GRIFFITHS

HOLDING THE CUE

The easiest way of explaining how to grip the cue is to lay it on the table and then simply pick it up. Although I use the word 'grip' here, it should be much more of a relaxed but firm hold, using the front part of the hand, that is the thumb and first two fingers. Your other two fingers should be used not so much to hold the cue but to help with the balance, supporting it and keeping it in a straight line. The fingers must be kept together, with your thumb round the cue and resting on your forefinger.

Make sure you have enough control over the cue without squeezing it. If you do grip it too tightly, the muscles in your hand and wrist will tighten up and this in turn will stiffen the arm. When this happens you will never achieve the smoooth cue action required when you come to play the shot.

You will find that you do start to squeeze the cue as you go through with the shot, so you do not want your grip to be too tight before you start. If you do, you will lose that flexibility essential for a clean, accurate strike on the cue ball.

Having said that, you equally don't want to hold the cue too loosely, since you will not achieve the desired control when you hit the cue ball. Remember that every shot needs to be played with a firm, positive action, even if you want the softest of touches on the cue ball.

The size of your hand can affect the way you grip and so this is a very good way of testing whether you have the right cue. Your hand should always feel comfortable around the butt. So if you have small

The 'grip' on the cue must be firm but relaxed. You need good control without squeezing your hand round the butt end. Note here how the line of the knuckles is parallel to the floor with the cue in the rest position. This is a good way of checking your hand is in the correct position.

hands you need a smaller butt – and a larger one with bigger hands.

One good way of checking the position of your hand for the basic grip is with the line of the knuckles. This should be parallel to the floor and in line with the cue when you are in the rest position. This will obviously change slightly for the back swing and follow-through, as I will come to later.

Normally the wrist should be in the vertical position, although the important thing is that it remains firm and does not wobble. In fact Steve actually cocks his wrist outwards slightly to lock it in with his arm.

The exact position of the hand on the cue will vary and I do not feel this is necessarily critical for your cue action. Of course, if you have to hold the cue too far down, then this indicates that the cue is too long for you.

The normal position is an inch or so from the end. Some players allow a little more. Steve, for example, holds his cue about three inches from the end. It is important to allow yourself some room for manoeuvre, since for certain shots you will need to alter the length of your back swing.

To help achieve maximum back swing for a power shot – or when I am bridging at full stretch, I move my grip to the end of the cue, in which case I tuck my little finger round the back of the butt. Some people actually find this position more comfortable, anyway. In contrast, when I am playing a very soft shot and just want to roll the cue ball, I will shorten my grip, moving it slightly more down the cue to limit the back swing. But more on this later.

The golden rule with any grip is to make sure that you have good control over the cue and can play every shot firmly and positively. Although the exact strength of the grip will vary slightly from player to player, it should never be too tight or too loose. Within this allowance, Tony and Neal for example tend to have a tighter grip while in contrast Dennis's grip is a bit slacker. But in all cases they retain firm control over the cue and its movement.

TAKING UP POSITION

As you will find out very quickly, there is no point in rushing up to the table and just hitting the balls in the hope that, because you have seen a shot that is on, it is bound to go in. The right preparation

It is important that your hand feels comfortable around the butt of the cue and this will affect the size of cue you get. You can see here how my hand fits well round the butt – firmly, but not too tight.

is absolutely critical to the success of any shot and you must take time to get this absolutely right.

When you approach the table, you need to study the position of the balls and consider carefully what shot you want to play. You will notice that invariably we will walk round and have a look at the different options available and, possibly, even test out a particular shot. Sometimes, of course, we will be looking at possible positions for subsequent shots. But this preparation is essential and should never be hurried.

Only when you have decided on the shot you want to play should you take up your position at the table and get down to play the shot. And I must stress that this is a very strict and necessary order to follow. You will often see an inexperienced player get down for a shot and then shuffle around as he makes up his mind exactly what he is going to do. Make up your mind first and then get down in the right position.

So what is the right position? Obviously this is determined by the line of the shot you have decided to play. I will be talking about sighting the shot later, but this is something that will come as fairly difficult

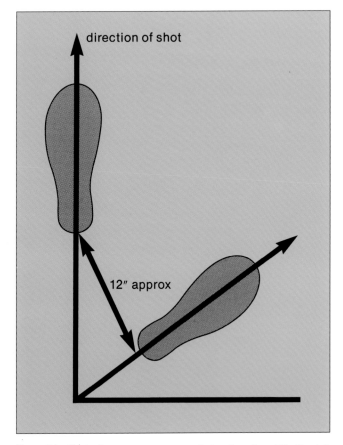

direction of shot

12″ approx

From this illustration, you can see the correct position of the feet when getting down for the shot. The right foot should be placed in line with the shot, but angled outwards, while the left foot is forward, about 12 in away and pointing in the direction of the shot.

at first. With experience, however, you will do it automatically.

It also depends on the type of shot you are going to play, which is why you need to have decided on whether you are going to attack or defend, play a power shot or just stroke the ball. In snooker, decisions have to be made first before you set up for the shot. Apart from the stance you adopt, this is important since it then leaves you clear to concentrate on the shot you want to play.

Having said this, any decision you make at this stage is not irrevocable. If you feel, when you get down at the table, that you are not happy with the shot – or your position, for that matter – you should

get up from the table and start the whole process again. We do this even at a professional level, although sometimes we are accused of slow play. At the end of the day it is the shot you play that counts, not how long it takes you to play it.

So what is the correct stance to adopt? If you study each of the Matchroom players – or any other professional, for that matter – you will see that each is slightly different. If you watch a lot of the tournament snooker you can probably tell who is who just by the way they stand, which goes to prove how different individual stances can be.

The important point about any stance is that it must be solid and comfortable, while at the same time allowing the cue to travel back and forward in a straight line. When you come to play a shot, the only part of your body that should move is your cueing arm. Everything else should be kept perfectly still.

The exact angle of the body in relation to the table will vary slightly from person to person. Steve, for example, adopts quite a square-on stance, since he finds this helps him resist any sideways movement. Other players stand more directly in line with the shot.

The most important aspect of the stance is the position of your feet. To start with, you need to be the correct distance from the table and this will of course depend on your height and reach. You must make sure that your weight is slightly forward on to your bridging hand and you can easily test this by lifting this hand off the table, which should send your body forward. This is achieved by having your left foot further forward than your right one (or vice-versa if you are a left-handed player).

Again taking the example of a right-handed player, your right foot should be on the same line as that of the shot, with the toes angled outwards slightly. The left foot should be at least 12 in. away from the right to ensure a firm base and solid, rigid stance, with the toes pointing in the same direction as the line of the shot. For all normal shots, both feet should remain firmly on the floor.

You should always keep the right leg straight, since this must act as a brace for the rest of your body. Depending on your height, you will have to bend your left leg slightly to help bring the weight forward and ensure your cue is horizontal to the floor. This will, of course, be restricted by the height of the

cushion. The shorter you are, the straighter your left leg will tend to be.

As a general rule, you should keep your stance as much sideways on as possible to ensure all the relevant parts of the body are in line with the shot. At the same time you must allow yourself sufficient room for a free-flowing cue action, both back and forwards, without touching your body.

Imagine with your stance that you are forming a tripod, using your legs and the bridging hand. Achieving the right balance is most important, since if you are too far back the weight will be in the

Above: You can see clearly here the position I adopt, the distance I stand from the table, the position of the feet and the fact that while my right leg is straight, the left leg is bent slightly. This is important to adjust the height of the stance and ensure the cue is parallel to the floor.

Right: From the back, you will notice the position of the feet, with the left foot pointing in the direction of the shot and the right foot placed in line with the shot but angled outwards.

opposite direction to the shot, while if you are too far forward you will be putting more weight over the shot. This will not only be uncomfortable, but will also cramp your cue action.

From this series of photographs (to p 31) you can compare the
stances of all the Matchroom players. You will see how the position of
the bridge in relation to the cue ball varies between players. But the
one thing we all have in common is that the cue is always as parallel as
possible to the floor, with the head well down. This is very important. It
is particularly noticeable how far Willie, the tallest of the Matchroom
team, stands from the table.

Here Steve is slightly closer to the table, an adjustment he has made quite recently. Noticeably his left hand is nearer the cue ball and to allow for this he has brought his right hand up the cue a little.

Naturally for a left-handed player, such as Jimmy is, the stance is reversed, with the right leg forward and bent slightly to bring the weight forward. Otherwise the same basic principles apply.

Of all the Matchroom players, Tony stands closest to the table, with his head right over the edge. Obviously the shorter you are the nearer you should be to the table.

Dennis stands fairly well back from the table and bends his left leg
considerably to bring himself forward into the shot when cueing up.

Neal is one of the tallest of the Matchroom team but stands reasonably close to the table. Note how his left arm is stretched well out towards the cue ball.

FORMING THE BRIDGE

Remember that your bridging hand has a vital role to play in controlling the cue through the full action and must therefore be as firm as possible and remain that way. The slightest movement of this hand could affect the contact you make with the cue ball and the accuracy of the strike.

To form the bridge, spread your hand out over the table, with your fingers as wide apart as possible. Then push your finger pads down on the cloth and cock your thumb to create as deep a 'V' shape as you can, squeezing it close to your forefinger. I am fortunate in that my thumb bends back naturally and Steve's thumb is double-jointed so he can cock it up very high to create a good deep groove for the cue. You will have to see what your thumb can achieve!

Of course, everyone has a different size and shape of hand. Those with larger hands and thick fingers will naturally tend to have a higher bridge. This then has to be adjusted for certain shots, particularly when creating back spin on the cue ball. This will be covered later.

I have small hands and thin fingers and naturally bridge lower, which is of course ideal for back spin shots. I can raise the bridge to a degree by gripping the cloth more, which automatically brings up the knuckles. To lower the bridge, you should raise the outside of your hand slightly, but keep the inside firmly on the table.

As with all forms of bridge, the more contact your hand has with the table, the better the bridge will be.

Having stressed that the bridged hand must be as firm and still as possible throughout the cue action, someone is bound to ask why Tony gets away with his twitching middle finger. Well, if you try it you will notice that this does not affect any other part of the hand and everything else remains perfectly still. And Tony assures me that he does not even notice he is doing it. It is simply a nervous, involuntary movement. All I can say is that you certainly do not want to develop anything like that, but equally should not worry if it happens!

Having established a firm bridge, where should this be in relation to the cue ball? Measuring from the 'V' of your thumb, your bridge should be between 9 in. and 12 in. from the cue ball. The exact distance will depend on the position of the cue ball and where

These three views of my bridged hand show clearly how this should be formed. The hand is spread over the table with the fingers as wide apart as possible. You can see here how with a normal bridge I have got maximum contact with the table through my fingers, with the hand arched to ensure the cue comes through at the right level for a plain ball shot. The thumb is well cocked to provide a deep grove through which the cue can travel. Naturally the exact bridge you form will depend on the size and shape of your hand and how flexible your joints are.

other balls are in relation to it.

The shorter the bridge, the more you will restrict the movement of the cue and the less back swing you will achieve. As you will discover later, a full back swing is particularly important when playing power shots. Equally the closer the bridge is to the cue ball, within reason, the more accurate your strike should be, since you are reducing the margin for error.

The size of your hand or length of your fingers is not relevant here, since you are looking at the distance from the 'V'. What you need to make sure is

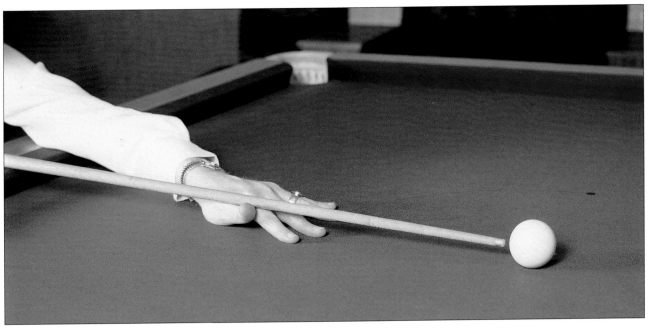

From the front and back views here you can see my position in the stance in relation to the shot. Note how the left arm is slightly bent. From the back you will notice how the right foot is in the direct line of the shot.

that you are, where possible, bridging the minimum comfortable distance from the cue ball for the type of shot you want to play.

One final point here worth remembering is that the closer the bridge is to the cue ball, the harder it becomes to sight the ball. And because another guide to accurate sighting is the movement of your cue back and forward, the more room between the bridge and cue ball for the cue to travel the easier it is to check for any error.

I have obviously concentrated on the ideal bridging position and there will be times when this proves impossible, either because the cue ball is too close to the cushion or, for example, there is another ball in the way. Variations for awkward bridging are covered later.

In talking about the bridge, we have not yet discussed the position of the left arm, which again varies from player to player. The traditional school of thought was that the left arm should always be thrust forward in as straight a line as possible. Personally I have my left arm bent slightly and resting on the table because it gives my bridged hand a lot more stability. Steve does the same, partly for that extra support but also because, being tall, he found a straight left arm tended to cramp his cueing action.

The best way to find out what suits you is to practise with the left arm straight and then bent and see if there is any difference. The most important factor is that you feel comfortable, have a solid bridge and can at the same time move your cue freely in line with the shot.

I should finally mention here that there are occasions when players do vary the distance from the bridge to the cue ball. Both Steve and I tend to do this when we are playing a particularly soft shot. Then we may come in as close as 4 or 5 in. and bend the left arm more. The effect of this is to cut down the back swing and increase the accuracy of the shot. Obviously this is the principle of playing a more gentle shot.

The advantage of moving closer is that you do not have to think about reducing the back swing, since it happens automatically.

STRIKING THE BALL

INTRODUCTION BY STEVE DAVIS

I remember that when I first began to develop an interest in the game, the only snooker of any quality I could watch was Pot Black, which was shown once a week on television. My father and I would sit there on a Wednesday night, glued to the set for 25 minutes, watching every shot and trying to work out what it was that made the players so good at the game.

The one thing that did come across, even on television, was the positive way in which they hit the ball. It is difficult to describe, but they struck it very cleanly and precisely, crisply with a lot of authority. When they hit the ball, it was like a punch and the cue ball seemed to do whatever they wanted it to, obviously because they knew exactly what they were doing.

This is really the key to developing your game and becoming a good player - having that authority in the way you hit the ball. In the average player, this is often missing, either through lack of ability or possibly poor co-ordination of the arm. It can also be because they have not been shown the correct amount of back swing for different types of shot or for their own build. They need somebody to watch them and point out if they are bringing the cue back too far or not far enough or to highlight a fault in the cueing action itself. Often, of course, it is basically through a lack of confidence.

In this section, Terry describes the series of techniques involved in cueing correctly and striking the ball with that authority. Together with studying this, one of the best ways of appreciating the importance of this part of the game is to watch top players in action, preferably at a local tournament or exhibition where you can get quite close to them. By watching a good player striking the ball well, you can get a mental picture of the whole action which will complement what you have read in this book. Together these should help you improve the vital technique of positive striking.

STRIKING THE BALL

BY TERRY GRIFFITHS

Having mastered all the aspects of preparation – cue grip, stance and basic bridging – so that you can cope with each stage automatically almost without thinking about them, you must then concentrate on striking the cue ball correctly. This means bringing your cue through in a straight line and making exactly the contact you want with the cue ball for the shot you have selected.

This may not sound particularly difficult, but there is probably as much technique involved in this vital sequence as in any other aspect of playing snooker. For it is one thing to make accurate contact with the cue ball and quite another to do this consistently – in fact, with every shot you play.

Before I get on to the different elements that make up the complete cueing action, I must stress again the importance of keeping absolutely still on the shot. Only the right arm, wrist, eyes and, of course, the cue should move. The secret of successful cueing is having everything in line, which is easy enough when all your body is still. The problems start when you have to move your cue.

This is why it is so important to have mastered the basic technique of having your body in the correct position. For only then will you be able to isolate possible faults to those techniques involved in striking the cue ball. These can normally be traced back to incorrect sighting, your cue being off line or moving off line during delivery, but there could equally be something much more fundamentally wrong.

I will break the complete cueing action up into six sections - feathering, back swing, pause, hit, follow-through and stop. The first three you can, of course, look at and practise individually. The rest form one complete action and must be carried out together. Getting this complete sequence right is the key to perfect timing and therefore successful striking of the cue ball.

But first I want to look at the right arm and show you what this should be doing during the cueing action.

THE RIGHT ARM

Once you have set yourself up for the shot, the right arm becomes the most important part of your body, since at this stage it is the only moving part that controls the cue through the strike.

You should certainly try to get your right arm in as straight a line as possible with that of the shot. Some players, such as Steve, manage to have it dead straight and this is ideal because then the cue should automatically move in the same straight line. Of course there has to be a degree of tolerance. I know that my right arm is almost in line whereas with others, such as Ray Reardon and Cliff Thorburn, you can see the elbow sticking out. Obviously they are able to make the necessary adjustment to ensure that the cue still travels in a straight line with that of the shot.

You will find that if you tuck your elbow in, you tend to move the cue forward in an arc and end up striking the cue ball on the left. With the elbow out, the tendency is to hit the cue ball on the right. You may develop a style in which you can make the necessary adjustments. But you will find it easier to get the right arm as straight as you can. For one thing, it is less likely to let you down if you are under pressure or not playing as well as you might.

As I mentioned earlier when looking at the grip, the forearm should hang vertically when you are at the rest position. This provides you with the optimum back swing and follow-through while keeping the cue running parallel throughout the cueing action.

If it is slightly forward, this will give you a longer back swing, but equally will shorten the follow-through and the tendency will be to raise the cue off your bridge as you strike the cue ball. The reverse situation, with the forearm slightly backward, will restrict the back swing and the tendency will be to lift the butt of the cue. On the hit you will probably scoop with the cue and strike the ball too high. In either case, the only possible adjustment is to lower or raise your elbow, which not only makes the cueing action more complicated but increases the chance of error.

FEATHERING

What we call feathering is the initial stage of the full cueing action, the build-up to actually hitting the cue ball. Basically it is the process of addressing the ball. Whatever the type of shot you are playing, feathering is essential to help you establish a rhythm and get your timing right.

Your feathers should start from the rest position,

that is with the right arm in the vertical position and the cue as near parallel to the table as possible. You should then move the cue forward so the tip is as close as you dare get it to the cue ball without touching it.

It is interesting to note that, when you have mastered the art of feathering, if you are playing well you tend to get very close to the cue ball. In contrast, when you are not right on top of your game you are more likely to hold back a bit. Basically it is a matter of confidence and judgement. But it is important to get as close as you can, because this offers the maximum opportunity for getting the rhythm and timing right. The shorter your feathers, the less chance you are giving yourself.

Exactly how many times you feather will depend on how long it takes you to prepare yourself for the shot. What is important, I feel, is that you feather the same way every time. You should not, however, dwell too long on the feathers since you will eventually lose concentration and may be putting undue strain on your bridge, particularly if you are having to adopt an awkward one.

The exact number and length of feathers does vary from player to player. Mine have always been fairly long, although in recent years I have tended to shorten them somewhat. In fact, I have the longest of all the Matchroom players. Next comes Steve and Dennis, while Tony, Jimmy, Willie and Neal all feather very short. Normally, the shorter the feather, the less of a back swing you create, although this will vary according to the type of shot you are playing.

When you start to practise feathering, do not worry too much if you hit the cue ball occasionally. It is better to begin too long and to adjust back a little than always to feather short of the ball. And during this action, which must be as smooth as possible, make sure you keep absolutely still, with your head well down and the cue coming through in a straight line on to the cue ball.

THE BACK SWING

When you have completed your feathering and are absolutely ready to play the shot, you bring the cue back. How far will depend on the strength you need for that stroke. As will be discussed later, it is the length of back swing rather than any additional force in the strike that gives you the extra power you need.

As you draw the cue back, you will notice a slight change in the grip, as the wrist pivots slightly and the line of the knuckles becomes fractionally angled. You will find it impossible to keep everything in the horizontal position, particularly with a maximum back swing, but it is very important that you only adjust these two parts of the grip. You should never raise your shoulder to draw back the cue.

Obviously the longer the back swing the more chance there is of errors creeping in to the cueing action, because the cue then has to travel that much further forward into the shot. This is why some experts will tell you to limit the back swing to reduce the possibility of mistakes. Personally, I think this is the wrong approach, since you will automatically be limiting the range of shots available.

Naturally you should never bring the cue back further than you have to, but if you need maximum back swing for a power shot, you should go for it. This will encourage you to perfect your cueing action, rather than limit yourself because of an imperfect technique.

If you do shorten your back swing, there is a great tendency to force the cue through more quickly for a power shot. In this situation you are far more likely to push the cue off line and snatch at the cue ball because you will have upset the natural rhythm and timing of the delivery.

The back swing is a very important part of your cueing action, since it determines what happens to the cue when you bring it forward into the shot. If you complete the back swing in the wrong position, then you can be pretty certain the hit and follow-through will be wrong, too.

A final word on the length of your back swing. You will notice that professionals do not normally use a long back swing, except when playing power shots. This is because the tables they play on are generally of much better quality and faster. Therefore they do not need so much strength in the shot to make the ball travel across the cloth.

Club tables are usually that much slower and you will almost certainly find you have to lengthen your back swing to ensure you achieve the desired pace on the cue ball.

THE PAUSE

You must make it a golden rule to pause at the end of the back swing before moving into the final stroking sequence. If you do not, you will find it virtually impossible to maintain the correct rhythm, timing and control in the shot.

Probably the best way of looking at this stage of the cueing action is to imagine driving a car in reverse and then suddenly putting in into a forward gear. The change of direction would be too sudden if carried out with no pause.

The length of this pause is not critical and in fact only lasts a split second. But it should be there. One advantage is that it gives you that extra moment to concentrate your eyes on the object ball and, of course, once you are through the pause you are totally committed to playing the shot.

Of the Matchroom players, Steve tends to pause the longest, both Neal and I noticeably so, while the rest do so just for a fraction. But in all cases, it is there. Whatever you do, however, you must not pause for too long or you will tend to hesitate and upset your concentration and rhythm.

SIGHTING THE SHOT

While this procedure should not interrupt the sequence of the cueing action, it is very important to have established by this stage exactly what your eyes should be doing. That is why I mention it here, although you would naturally continue straight on to the final sequence of the hit, follow-through and stop.

You will have already established the line of the shot, since that will determine the exact position you take up at the table. This is, of course, the direction you intend to send the cue ball to hit the object ball. How exactly you decide on where on the object ball to aim will be discussed in the section on potting, which comes later.

The first thing you must concentrate on is being able to strike the cue ball cleanly and send it across the table in a straight line. If you don't master this basic technique, then you will never pot a ball consistently.

When sighting the shot, you must get your head centrally over the cue and as low as possible, prefer-

ably with your chin touching the cue. And you must learn to sight with both eyes. This highlights the importance of the side-on stance, since you should end up with your right arm, head and sighting all in the same line – along the cue.

At this stage, you should be looking along the cue to the spot on the cue ball you intend to hit. Once you start feathering, you follow this line of sight through the cue ball and on to that part of the object ball you want the cue ball to hit. You then flick your eyes from the cue ball to the object ball a few times just to double-check where you are hitting.

A fatal mistake that many people make is to concentrate on where the object ball is going, for example, towards a pocket. From the line of shot you have adopted, you have already determined this and the object ball will naturally follow that direction as long as the cue ball strikes it correctly. So all you need now concern yourself with is striking the cue ball accurately on to the object ball.

During the back swing your eyes should have settled on the cue ball and then started moving along to the object ball. From the pause, right through the hit and follow-through – and even up to the stop – they must be concentrating on that part of the object ball you intend to hit. The principle behind this is quite simply that you will naturally send the cue in the direction you are looking – that is in a straight line to the object ball.

So the golden rule, as all top players will tell you, is to have your eyes on the part of the object ball you want the cue ball to hit by the time the tip of your cue strikes the cue ball. What does vary is the precise stage at which your eyes reach this position – and that is all to do with individual timing.

Overleaf: This sequence shows the complete cueing action in stages, from the rest position to the back swing and then forward to the hit and follow-through. Notice how the back swing changes according to the type of shot you are playing. With a gentle shot, the right arm comes back only slightly, whereas it is brought back the full extent when playing a power shot. This will be covered in more detail later in the book. At the rest position, the right arm must be vertical and the cue parallel to the floor. Even in the back swing, the cue must remain as parallel as possible. The same applies with the follow-through, where you can see how far the cue has travelled through the cue ball. Notice how the right arm has dropped from its original position and, most importantly, that the chin is still on the cue, with the head well down over the shot.

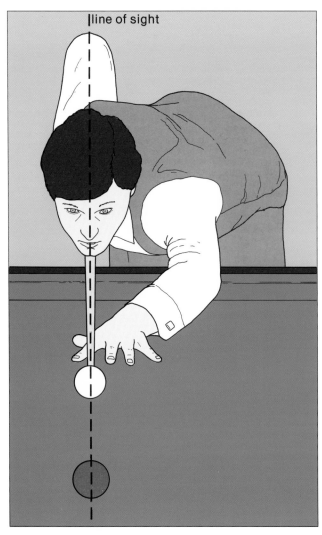

line of sight

From this illustration you can see clearly how you should be positioned when lining up the shot. Your head must be well down over the cue and centrally in line with cue ball and object ball. Make sure, too, that your right arm is in the same straight line with the cue.

Here I have lined up for the shot and you can see, as with the illustration, that my right arm, head and cue are all in the same straight line of the shot, through the cue ball to the object ball. This is crucial for accurate cueing.

Certainly of all the Matchroom players, Steve gets his eyes on to the object ball earlier than anyone. The rest of us tend to flick our eyes between the two balls more before we settle on the object ball.

I have always believed that this almost imperceptible action reflects whether a player is on good or bad form. When your timing is perfect, your eyes are on to the object ball that much earlier, while you still have half the cue ball in your sight.

This is not an easy thing to do and I still find it difficult to move to the object ball earlier, although I have certainly tried to because I am sure it would benefit me.

I will try to illustrate, in an exaggerated way, why it is so important to look at the object ball rather than the cue ball. If your eyes are on the cue ball when you strike it, the natural instinct is to follow its path up to the object ball. As your eyes move up, so there is a tendency to move your head, albeit only fractionally. This can cause a chain reaction and you find you are lifting your cue as well. If your eyes are firmly fixed on the object ball, then there is no reason to move them during and after the strike.

The secret to all this is confidence. When you are playing well and your timing is absolutely right, your eyes move naturally on to the object ball. It is when you are not playing so well that you tend to dwell on the cue ball to check on the strike and then move up to the object ball. There is often a reluctance to watch the object ball in case the shot goes wrong and you miss the pocket.

At no time during the cueing action sequence should your eyes deviate from the line between the cue ball and the part of the object ball you are aiming to hit. And even when the cue ball has struck the object ball, you should hold the position of your eyes and not follow the ball. Once you start to move your eyes, you will tend to do so earlier and earlier and eventually this could be before you strike the cue ball, which would be disastrous.

It is one of the most difficult habits to get into, but it is vital if you want to perfect your timing.

CUE DELIVERY

Having discussed what your eyes should be doing during the forward sequence of striking the ball, what about the cue itself? It doesn't matter what type of shot you are playing, whether a gentle roll or a full-blooded power shot. Your cue action into and through the strike must be positive.

To hit the cue ball successfully, you must make clean, firm contact with the cue tip and make sure you play through the ball. In fact, the cue should be moving at its maximum just after contact. What in effect you are doing is punching the ball rather than stabbing it.

During the hit and follow-through, as with feathering and the back swing, the only part of the body that should move is your right arm, which pivots at the elbow as your cue travels through the strike. All the

Here (up to p 46) you can see a similar sequence as before through the whole cueing action, showing a close-up of the grip, starting in the rest position. Note the arm position at each stage and the grip itself.

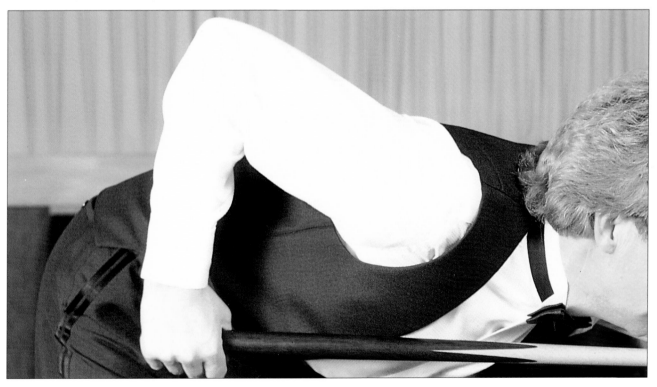

While the hand remains in virtually the same position on the back swing for a gentle shot as with the rest, the line of the knuckles is raised slightly the further back you bring the cue for a medium paced and full power shot.

time, the cue must remain on the same parallel plane and this is achieved by changing the position of the wrist slightly. During the hit it straightens out as the forearm comes through the vertical and then opens as you continue on with the follow-through.

The most common faults at the strike are that either the forearm has not reached the vertical position or that it has past it. This indicates that the player is either standing too close in relation to the cue ball or too far away. If the cue is not travelling through on a parallel plane, then it will be hitting down on the ball or on the rise.

How far you follow through after the strike will depend on what shot you are playing, as you will see later when variations on the plain ball are discussed. To a degree, it also depends on the individual. I use a long follow-through, as do Dennis and Neal, whereas Steve's, Jimmy's and Willie's are considerably shorter. In comparison, Tony has a very short cue action with virtually no follow-through at all. The answer is to practise varying the length of your follow-through to see what suits your cueing action best.

Although it is something you tend not to think about, you do, of course, have to stop the cue somewhere. Doing it at the right time for the right shot comes automatically for the top players, but it is nevertheless still part of the cueing action and the overall timing of the shot.

The speed at which the cue is travelling will affect where and when you stop it – as will the type of spin, if any, you are applying to the cue ball. Although this is covered later, I will just mention the principle since it helps to explain what happens when you stop your cue.

The amount of back spin you put on the cue ball will depend on how much 'bite' you get on it. Depending on when you stop the cue, you will get more or less 'hold' on the cue ball, which means that the earlier you stop the more back spin you will apply – and vice-versa. That is why for a plain ball shot you only stop the cue at the end of the follow-through.

It is important to remember, however, that the hit, follow-through and stop are all part of one complete action and should be practised as a whole. You cannot separate them. When you do go through with the shot, this must be a smooth action with every part of your body absolutely still, except of course your right arm. This includes your head, which should remain down even after the stop, to ensure the cue follows through accurately. There is little point at this stage looking up to see where the object ball has gone, since it is too late to do anything about it, anyway.

HITTING THE CUE BALL

Once you have mastered the technique of getting the cue to move back and forward in a straight line, using the cueing action I have explained here, then you can concentrate on hitting the cue ball in a straight line. It sounds easy – but I can assure you it takes months of practice to perfect and do consistently.

It is at this stage that you can start to develop the ideal strength in your striking of the cue ball, which does vary considerably from player to player. And this has got nothing to do with the height or build of a player, despite the fact that, of the Matchroom team, Steve, Jimmy and Neal tend to hit the ball the hardest.

Basically it is down to the individual cueing action which makes up a player's overall technique. Whereas Steve, Jimmy and Neal tend to punch the ball more, the rest of us are really touch players. As a result, we are more likely to make mistakes through mis-timing if we are slightly off form. You must decide for yourself which technique suits you best.

Left: The cueing action sequence ends with the hit and follow-through. Notice again the line of the knuckles and how straight the cue remains through the delivery.

Right: This is a very good way of practising your cue delivery and making sure the cue comes through in a dead straight line. Get down at the side of the table as if to play a shot along the baulk line. By going through the full cueing action, you can check to see that your cue is travelling along the baulk line. By cueing up with the tip on the brown spot, you can measure the amount of follow-through.

PRACTICE
CUE DELIVERY

You can practise your cue delivery, checking that it is moving backwards and forwards in a dead straight line, with the help of the baulk line at the bottom end of the table.

Standing at the side of the table, get down as if to play a shot with the tip of your cue on the brown spot. Then go through the full cueing action – feathers, back swing, pause, hit, follow-through and stop. Watch carefully to see whether your cue travels along the baulk line or whether it deviates at all.

The other advantage of this exercise is that you can measure how long your follow-through is – from the brown spot where you started to where the cue tip finishes up. This distance should be at least 3 or 4 in. Anything more than that is a bonus.

I suggest you practise this for at least five minutes before you go on to any other exercises to make sure you are cueing straight consistently.

This is a particularly useful exercise because you can do it on your own and don't need someone else there to watch what is happening to the cue.

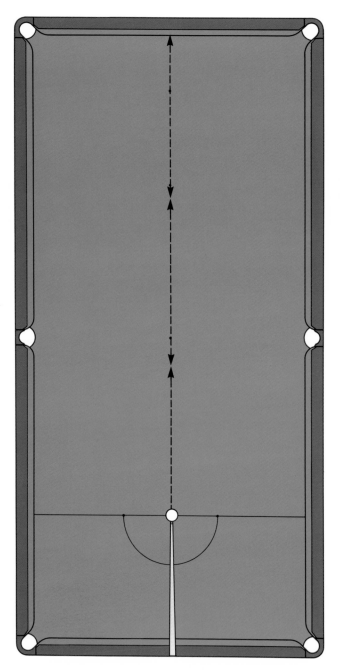

This exercise will show how straight you can hit the ball. Placing the cue ball on the brown spot, try hitting it up the table and back again. To ensure it runs over the spots in both directions, you need to hit it dead centre.

PRACTICE

STRAIGHT HITTING

This exercise is very important because it will demonstrate whether you have taken up the correct position at the table, whether your stance is right and also whether your cueing action is absolutely straight in line with the shot.

Place the cue ball on the brown spot. What you are planning to do is to strike this dead centre and send it up the table over the blue, pink and black spots and then back off the top cushion over the same spots so that it rolls over the brown spot again.

You will soon see if you are not hitting absolutely straight in the centre, because the cue ball will not run over the spots. And if, after hitting the top cushion, it comes back to the left or right of the spots, then you have in fact put side on it – that is, not struck it dead centre.

This is a very difficult exercise to do accurately every time, but it is absolutely vital if you are to hit the ball straight consistently. So don't be annoyed if you aren't successful first time. It needs hours and hours of practice.

And don't force the pace straight away. Begin by playing at medium strength and then, as you master it, you can increase the pace of the shot to a maximum. You won't always get the cue ball to run back over the brown spot, but it should be within an inch or so every time.

STRAIGHT HITTING WITH TWO BALLS

The next stage in practising straight hitting is to use two balls. With the cue ball on the brown spot, as before, place the blue ball in the same central line up the table about a foot away from the cue ball. Playing in exactly the same way, practise hitting the cue ball on to the blue ball and send it up the table over the spots and back down again to kiss the cue ball.

One of the problems with straight hitting is that it gets harder the further away the cue ball and object ball are. So after you have mastered this exercise, try the same shot but with the blue ball on its spot.

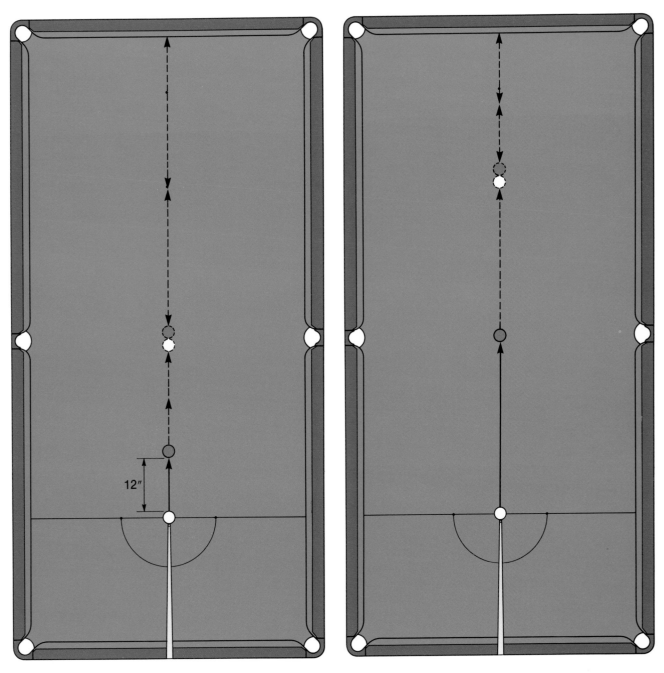

When you have mastered straight hitting with one ball, you can practise with two balls. Put the blue ball about 12 in up from the brown spot in the same central line and then hit the cue ball dead centre. The blue ball should run through the spots and back, kissing the cue ball in the middle of the table.

This exercise is similar to the last, but here you are playing the blue ball from its spot. The further away the object ball is, the harder it is to maintain absolutely straight hitting. The two balls should kiss somewhere near the pink spot.

POTTING THE BALL

INTRODUCTION BY STEVE DAVIS

Neal Foulds burst on to the snooker scene during the 1986/87 season, leaping in the world rankings from 13 to 3. One of the reasons for this was that for spells during the season he never missed a pot. It was as if every pocket had a magnet inside, particularly when he went for long pots, which were going in all over the table.

Obviously, if your long potting is good, your short potting will be excellent. And this is the supreme test of accuracy, since the longer the shot, the more chance there is of errors creeping in. Neal showed that not only was he able to get the long pots, but he could do so with screw back, follow-through etc. It never seemed to matter where the balls were on the table; he had the ability to maintain the highest degree of accuracy.

I believe a big reason for this was that Neal was in the right frame of mind. To be able to pot well, you have to be in a very positive frame of mind, because there is usually a considerable element of danger in the shot. If you miss the pot, you are likely to leave your opponent in for a simple shot afterwards. In Neal's case, his attitude was so good; he felt right within himself. Although he was obviously aware that he would leave his opponent in if he missed, he also knew from a percentage point of view he was right to go for it. Because he had the right approach and was happy with his game, the pots went in more easily.

In a way, to be potting well and having no fear of missing the shot could be compared to a racehorse wearing blinkers. All it can see is what is in front of it. In snooker, you know the shot you have to play and you know the position you want to play to afterwards. What you musn't do is worry about the overall situation or the state of the table when you actually hit the ball. All your thoughts must be on potting that ball. In the same way a racehorse has to concentrate on passing the winning post first and not worrying about what the other horses are doing around it.

Throughout this section, Neal looks at the basic principles of potting and discusses how these link in with the earlier sections on technique. He also stresses the importance of going back to basics and starting again if you are not potting well. There is no simple, easy way of learning how to pot, despite what you may read in advertisements for potting aids. To master the art of potting you have to play as much as you can. Eventually your eye – and your memory – will tell you how. These are your only reliable potting aids.

I hear many players round the country saying: "I'm okay when it comes to potting balls at an angle; I can judge these all right. But I can't get the straight ones, particularly the longer shots." What they are in fact saying is that they haven't got their technique right. What this is highlighting is that the cue is not going through into the shot consistently straight. Over a period a regular player learns to judge angles. But with straight pots no judgement is required, just very accurate cueing. Where you miss these, your cueing technique is not strong enough.

Nothing will put an opponent off more than consistent, aggressive potting – and this is an area in which Neal excels when he's on form. I can assure you that this can frighten the life out of other players if they are not careful. This is of course dependent on great accuracy, but also having a balanced approach to shots. One thing you will notice about Neal is the difference in the way he tackles a difficult pot from an easy one. Some players get down and play every shot in a certain length of time, whatever the situation. One of Neal's great qualities is that when he has a difficult pot which requires particularly good technique, he will always give himself that extra bit of time to prepare before he gets down to play the ball. This is a very valuable lesson to learn and adopt.

POTTING THE BALL

BY NEAL FOULDS

Potting is, of course, the supreme test of all you have learnt in the basic techniques – lining up for the shot, the cueing action and hitting the cue ball in a straight line. Until you can achieve this consistently, you can never guarantee potting a ball and, after all, that is what the game of snooker is all about.

Although it is possible to discuss the principles of potting and to give advice on what you should and shouldn't be doing, you cannot actually teach anyone how to pot. This part of the game is all about natural ability; either you can do it or you can't. Having said that, you will improve your potting with practice and experience. Assuming that your basic cueing technique is right, then it is down to individual judgement as to whether you have worked out the potting angle correctly.

I must stress at this stage that deciding on the angle of the pot must be done before you get down to play the shot. When you are standing up, you get the best view of the table and where you need to send the object ball. And this, of course, will determine the exact position you take up at the table. Once you have got down for the shot, you will not have a complete view of the cue ball and object ball in relation to the pocket you have chosen.

But before I go on to talk about potting angles, it is absolutely essential that you can pot a ball in a straight line, since this shot is solely reliant on your cueing technique.

POTTING IN A STRAIGHT LINE

The advantage of practising straight potting is that, although you need to send the object ball on and into the pocket, you can forget about the direction it has to take. If you hit the cue ball in a straight line, the object ball is bound to go in, as long as you have lined the shot up correctly.

This means that you can concentrate on your cueing technique and, before the hit, on the centre of the object ball. This avoids the natural tendency of the beginner to worry about where the object ball is going and therefore to follow its movement once the cue ball has hit it.

You are bound to find in the early stages that you miss quite a lot of these straight pots. But instead of worrying whether you have got the potting angle

right, you can concentrate on the various aspects of the basic technique, because this is where the fault must lie. Possibly you didn't sight up the shot correctly or were not exactly in line – or your cue didn't come through straight on to the cue ball.

Straight pots always look so easy and people can never understand why they are missed. But even at the professional level we miss them because an error has crept in to our technique. It can happen to the best of players.

Some while ago I started having problems with the straight pots. It happened in a tournament against Terry, when I started missing long straight balls which are normally my favourites, even when they were only 3 ft or so. I worked out afterwards that the trouble stemmed from my right arm, which was hitting my chest on the way through. I was using a long bridge and my arm was obviously much nearer my chest than it would normally be. As it touched, it was moving out slightly and this was enough to put side on the cue ball. The result was that the object ball kept hitting the corner of the pocket instead of going in.

My solution was to shorten the bridge and alter my stance fractionally so that my body was more forward on the shot. This cured the problem.

I use this as an example to show that the reason I was missing straight pots was because of a fault in my technique, which I went away with and sorted out after the match. And this is an important point, too. Even if you know there is something wrong during a competitive game, that is not the time to put it right. You must keep going as best you can in the hope that it rectifies itself. The place to sort it out is on the practice table afterwards. If you start changing things there and then, you are just going to make matters even worse.

It is important to recognise when you are doing something wrong and be prepared to change it. This is why, although you must establish the basic techniques as already described, it is often necessary to make minor adjustments to suit your style of play. What may be right for one player isn't always the best for another.

I sorted out my problem by changing the position of my right foot so that it was in line with the shot and moved the left one over until it felt comfortable. With the straight pot it is basically a question of playing the cue ball as if the object ball wasn't there. All you have to do is strike the cue ball correctly in the middle, which I was unable to do because of the way I was standing.

I remember Terry pointing out to me afterwards that he also felt there was a lack of rhythm in my cueing action, particularly while I was feathering. Apparently I was stopping when the cue tip got near the ball and this in turn upset the rhythm of my eyes going from the cue ball to the object ball.

So you see how important it is to have all aspects of your basic technique working correctly all the time.

This is why I feel to start with you should practise playing straight pots as softly as possible. There is always a tendency, particularly with the longer pots, to hit the cue ball harder than you have to with the idea of stunning it. But this is where you make mistakes. You will find that by playing a soft shot the cue ball will usually stop where the object ball was anyway, depending on the distance it has to travel – and there is far less chance of forcing errors in your cueing action.

Some players always seem to generate power at any speed and maintain accuracy. Jimmy is a perfect example. In contrast, Steve is very economical and rarely uses more power for the shot than he needs. As good as his technique is, he knows that the more power in the shot, the more chance of error.

Hitting the cue ball correctly is, as I have said, vital for successful potting and an interesting habit I have noticed with Jimmy may be of help to those who have difficulty in striking the ball dead centre.

When he addresses the ball, he shapes to cue very low down, even when he is playing a normal 'run through' shot, and then moves the cue directly up from there. If you think about it, the best way of establishing the vertical centre of the ball is from its point of contact with the cloth. Where you hit the ball along the line is far less critical than hitting it to the left or right. Although it will alter the effect the ball has on contact with the object ball, it should still travel in a dead straight line. By hitting it to the left or right there is more chance of sending it off course slightly and consequently missing the pot.

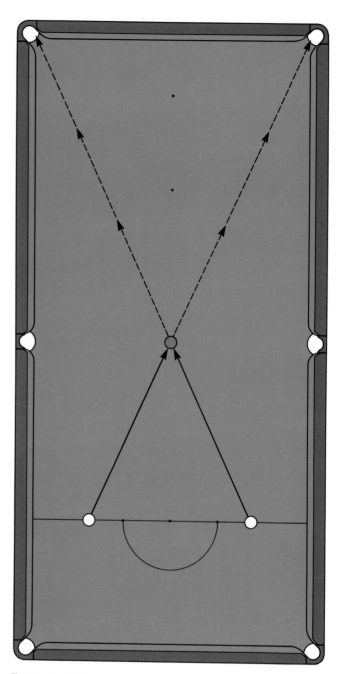

To practise potting in a straight line, place the blue ball on its spot and then line up the cue ball on the baulk line to give yourself a straight pot into each of the top corner pockets. It may look simple, but the distance involved makes it a harder shot to do consistently.

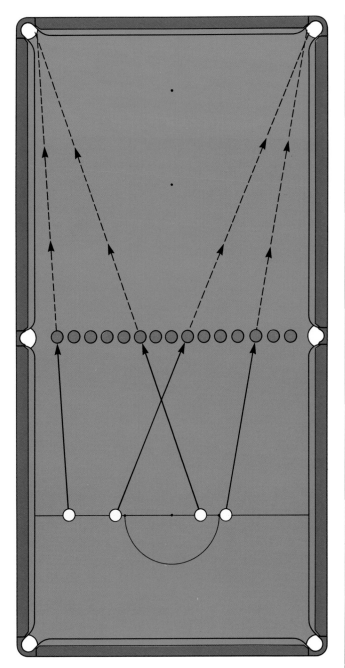

This is another, much more difficult practice for straight potting, which involves lining up all the reds across the middle of the table and potting each into either top pocket by placing the cue ball along the baulk line in a straight line with the chosen red and the pocket.

PRACTICE

POTTING IN A STRAIGHT LINE

One of my favourite practices is potting the blue on its spot with the cue ball on the baulk line, but positioned directly in line with either of the top pockets. This is a straight pot but made harder because of the distance the balls have to travel. You want to do 50 of these at a time, which will really test your cueing action.

When I turned professional I was potting about 40 out of the 50, which is a good average by any standards. To begin with you will not get anywhere near this, but you should be looking to get at least 30 to achieve any acceptable level of efficiency. Less than 25 and you must start looking at your basic technique to find out where you are going wrong.

There are times when I have got very few and I then have to check and see what is wrong with my action. Normally you will find that after 15 or 20 of these pots you get into a rhythm of potting without even looking at the shot.

There is a similar, but much harder, exercise that Steve does, where he lines all the reds up across the table between the two centre pockets. He then places the cue ball on the baulk line for each red, so that he has a straight long pot into one of the top corner pockets.

The reds nearest to the cushions are the hardest – and normally you will be lucky to get them to wobble in the jaws. Even Steve has yet to pot all the reds. That's how difficult it is.

POTTING FROM OFF THE CUSHION

This is a valuable exercise, because it helps you get used to striking the cue ball cleanly and accurately when it is against the cushion, thus also helping you to perfect awkward bridging.

With the black on its spot, put the cue ball in a direct line with the black and each of the top pockets in turn and try potting the black. You can then move the cue ball up and down the cushion to give you a range of angles on the black.

You will find this situation does occur quite a lot when you are playing round the black ball and will give you tremendous advantage in a break if you can master it.

POTTING AT AN ANGLE

Although with an angled pot you have to send the object ball in a different direction to the line of sight, the basic principle of hitting the cue ball straight still applies. In this respect, nothing has changed as far as the cueing action and lining up is concerned. The only difference is that you will not be aiming to make contact dead centre on the object ball.

Working out angles is simply down to judgement and experience, which after a while experienced players do not even have to think about. Having looked at the position of the balls, they know exactly what angle is needed to pot a particular ball.

You must work out the angle of the pot before you get down for the shot, since this will determine your position at the table and the line of sight you adopt. If you find when you get down that you are not in quite the right position, you must get up and start again. Never shuffle about, move your feet or alter the position of your bridge since this will almost certainly upset the cueing action and therefore the shot.

One of the easiest ways of establishing this is to think about where you would approach the table for a straight pot, since this is the easiest position to work out, and then concentrate on where in relation to this you need to stand in order to get the correct angle on the object ball to send it into the pocket. Having got down in this position, you will have automatically set your potting angle.

So what about the potting angle? On the face of it, you would probably think there were innumerable different angles and therefore any reasonable calculations were quite impractical. In fact, there are basically three main potting angles you should concentrate on, naturally making minor adjustments as required.

Working from a full-ball contact, which would in effect be a straight pot, you have threequarter-ball, half-ball and quarter-ball contacts. The extreme situation would be a fine cut, where you literally clip the very edge of the object ball.

You should work hard at recognising these angles since every pot you play for will come within this range, with possibly a slight variation either way, by playing a fraction thicker or thinner as required.

To begin with, you will probably need a point of reference when trying to work out angles for the pot.

The best way is to imagine a straight line from the object ball into the middle of the pocket. Carrying this line through to the outer edge of the object ball, it is here that the cue ball should make contact.

You should not think of this as a specific spot on the object ball, since it would be impossible to aim the cue ball at this with any reasonable degree of accuracy. It is far better, if you can, to imagine the cue ball superimposed on the object ball, with both balls in line with the pocket. This is best explained in the illustration, where you can see how, with a full, threequarter, half and quarter-ball pot, the cue ball would be positioned in relation to the object ball.

With the three main potting angles, what you should be looking for when you sight up the line of the shot is the cue ball covering threequarters, half or a quarter of the object ball – or, of course, fractional variations of these positions.

The value of thinking in terms of these three angles is that you can then recognise roughly the angle you require for potting – and of course this applies wherever the balls are positioned on the table. It is then down to experience, memory and judgement as to whether you need to play the angle a fraction thicker or thinner.

One thing you will find when working out the angle is that this becomes harder the closer together the cue ball and object ball are. Although the principle is still the same, the extra distance between the balls seems to make the calculation that much easier. In this situation I try to imagine the cue ball further away from the object ball in order to work out the correct angle and then move closer in with the shot, keeping the same angle on the object ball.

One way of practising potting angles is to place the cue ball in a plant situation against the object ball, that is when both balls are lining up together with the pocket. Note the position of the cue ball then take it away and play it on to that position.

There is no easy way of working out the potting angles and you should certainly discount any theories such as playing to where the light reflects off the object ball. It all boils down to experiment and experience.

The extreme angle is the fine cut, a shot that many people find hard to judge. This is not surprising, since you have almost got to aim to miss the object ball. But it is incredible how far you can cut a ball back. As

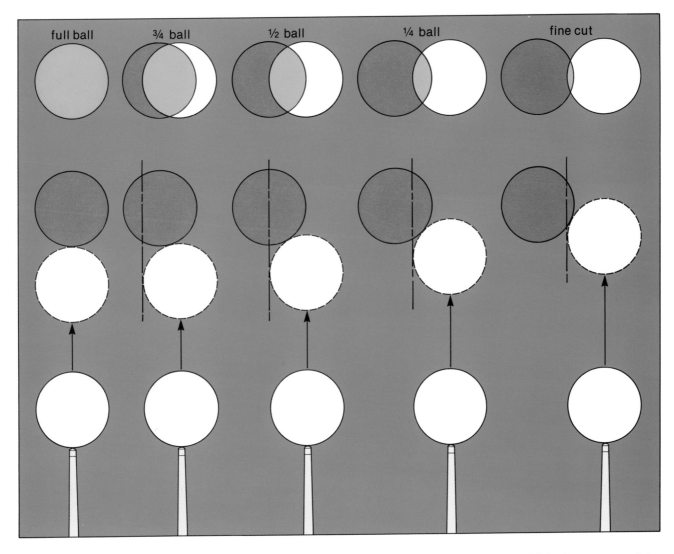

full ball	¾ ball	½ ball	¼ ball	fine cut

Here you can see the five basic types of contact between the cue ball and the object ball, including the three main potting angles – threequarter, half and quarter-ball. With a full-ball shot the area of contact on the object ball, indicated by the shaded area, is of course the whole ball.

With a threequarter-ball shot, you will be aiming to make contact with threequarters of the object ball, half with a half-ball shot and a quarter with a quarter-ball shot. The area of contact for a fine cut will naturally vary, but is always just a fraction of the object ball.

an experiment, you can try potting the black off its spot into the left-hand top pocket with the cue ball on the yellow spot. Having seen this angle, would you believe that it is also possible to cut it into the

right-hand top pocket? I wouldn't, however, advise anyone to try this out in a match.

One of the best hitters of a thin pot is Dennis. The classic situation is where the cue ball is down by the baulk colours and just a few reds have been broken out from the pack. Dennis will not only pot one of these into one of the top pockets but do so with a sufficiently fine cut as to bring the cue ball back safely into baulk – just in case he missed the pot. The only worry here would be if the red rattled in the jaws of the pocket, leaving a simple pot for his opponent. Rex Williams was another master at this.

This type of shot will be discussed in more detail when Dennis looks at tactical play later in the book.

But it is worth mentioning here that he has quite a reputation as a cagey player. And that is partly because he is so good at judging an angle. There have been many occasions when, playing Dennis in a match, I thought I had left him in a spot of trouble. But it is as though he sees angles and shots that nobody else does, because he will not only play himself out of trouble but pot a ball for good measure.

Players tend to have favourite angles and would normally try to play to these. Willie is not called Mr 147 for nothing and this is partly because he has mastered all the angles off the black. It is certainly a rare occasion when Willie misses the black off its spot. Favourite angles vary, as I have said, based on the type of player you are. The more safety-minded prefer half-ball shots where the cue ball can run away safely. The more attacking player, such as Jimmy, Tony or Willie, would probably prefer more of a fuller angle.

The best way of telling what a player prefers is to watch where he places the cue ball for a long red, should it have dropped into a pocket. I am probably

Probably the best place to get used to the potting angles is round the black spot, since this is where you will want to concentrate your play during a break. This sequence (to page 59) gives you a player's view of the main potting angles on either side of the black, from quarter-ball to full-ball. The red ball has been placed in front of the black to indicate where on the black the cue ball should make contact. If you refer back to the earlier illustration showing the potting angles, you will see in each case the area of the object ball covered by the cue ball.

one of the few who would go for a straight pot, because that's the one I have practised a lot over the years and therefore prefer. Most would go for a threequarter-ball pot.

The more you play, you will eventually work out the angles you prefer and are best at. Obviously you need to have reached quite an advanced stage to be able to control this and should anyway be able to cope with any angle. The secret is plenty of practice.

Having talked about angles on the object ball, the strange thing is that now I never think about the type of angle. I just know from its position in relation to the pocket where I need to hit it with the cue ball to pot it. I certainly don't think to myself: "This is a

To demonstrate how finely you can cut a ball, it is possible to pot the black off its spot into the top left-hand pocket with the cue ball on the yellow spot. But don't expect to pot the black first time!

half-ball or a quarter-ball.'' But it is important to think about this when you are starting to learn the angles. Hopefully, after a while, they will just come naturally.

My advice is to make sure you have a good look at the shot first before you get down to play it. Don't just walk up to the table and get down and guess on where to strike the object ball. And to start with it is always better to play the ball thicker rather than thinner. This is the advice my father used to give me when I first started playing. Particularly with long pots, you definitely feel you have more control over the shot. If you hit too thin, it tends to feel as though you are misjudging it.

I find that I do tend to hit balls a bit thick at times and this seems to have the same effect as applying a little side on the ball to help the object ball into the pocket. This will be discussed later. There are also times when you decide to play a slightly thicker or thinner contact to ensure good position for your next shot – or as a safety precaution. This is particularly so with a long pot, where if you did miss it at least with a thin contact you would bring the cue ball back down the table to a relatively safe position.

I have noticed, with good amateur players, that when they are off form they definitely play on the thick side. This is particularly obvious when attempting to pot the black on or near its spot, because they will want to stay on that colour if they can. They cannot do this if they have a thin contact.

Although this is not the place to be talking about positional play, since that comes later, it is worth mentioning here because I believe it has a lot to do with misjudging angles. How often have you seen a player miss the pot but gain perfect position for the next shot, or alternatively get the pot but lose position?

You have to decide which you would rather do. I know that I would rather get the pot and then necessarily play safe on the next shot because I had lost position. This is one of the main problems when you are developing your game. If you were able to set just one ball up, you would almost certainly pot it every time. But somehow with all the other balls around, this tends to complicate the shot and angles sometimes seem to change in your mind. You are then so concerned about the other balls that you miss the first and most important shot.

One of the best examples I can remember was a South African called Perrie Mans, who was a tremendous potter but not so good at positional play. He never used to worry about this, however, and took each shot as it came. In complete contrast, Willie is not only an excellent potter of the ball but currently the best player when it comes to building big breaks. And good positioning after each shot is vital if you want to put a good break together.

One of the most common faults when you do miss a pot is that you are concentrating too much on the pocket and not enough on the actual shot. Strangely enough, there are some professionals who do check on the pocket, usually during the back swing. Stephen Hendry does this; so does Cliff Thorburn. But I certainly would not recommend this practice, since you are liable to destroy your rhythm.

Once you have lined up the shot, you should not need to check it again since you know where the pocket is – and it's not going to move! Your rhythm is built up by looking from the cue ball to the object ball. If you then glance at the pocket this will only tend to distract you from the shot.

While on the subject of pockets, the point has already been made that these are cut differently, depending on the table. There are times when you have to adjust the pot to cope with this, which may mean aiming for the far jaw rather than the near one – or vice-versa. To do this, you will have to make a slight adjustment to your potting angle. Again, measuring this exactly only comes with lots of experience.

PRACTICE

JUDGING THE ANGLES

A useful exercise to do to start learning the angles – and one that Terry recommends – is to put the cue ball on the brown spot and position the blue ball about a foot away on the centre line up the table. Then practise striking the blue ball on each side, using different angles – ie threequarter, half and then quarter-ball. Each time you play a shot, watch where the blue ball hits the top or side cushion and try to remember this.

The sequel to this exercise is to try potting the blue ball from the same position into each of the top corner pockets in turn. To start with you will almost certainly miss. But if you note how far out you are each time and make the necessary adjustments you will start to pot the blue quite regularly.

POTTING THE BLACK

The most common exercise on the black, which helps you understand the basic angles, is to position it on its spot and set up seven reds in an arc. The first would be for a full-ball pot, and the three on either side for threequarter, half and quarter-ball pots. Working round the arc, above and below the black, you pot it using each red in turn.

Once you feel you have mastered the range of angles off the black, you can try a similar exercise but this time using the cue ball and potting from wherever it finishes up. Each time you respot the black and play into one of the top corner pockets.

These are very useful exercises because you should always be looking to score off the black when you can, particularly when the reds are still reasonably well clustered. If as professionals we miss a black, there really is little excuse. I don't think usually it is because we have hit it in the wrong place, so much as a slight technical error. I remember when I first started the game, I used to pot the black off its spot and run the cue ball through and see how many I could pot consecutively. This is a good idea to test how well you know your angles.

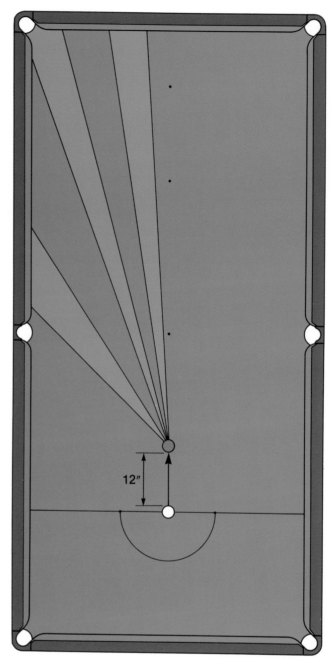

12″

A good way to get a feel for the different potting angles is to place the cue ball on the brown spot with the blue about 12in up the table. Then play the blue threequarter, half and then quarter-ball and watch where the blue goes, indicated here by the shaded bands. Try and remember the direction for each shot.

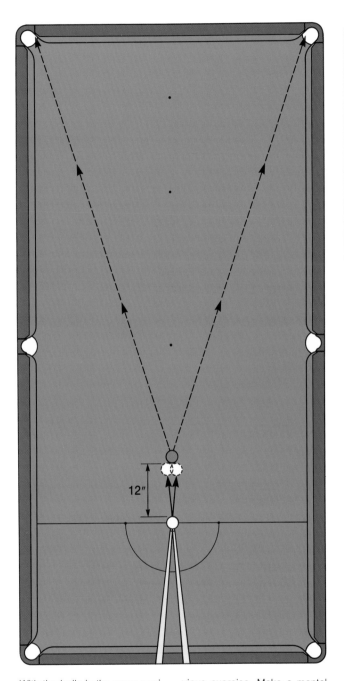

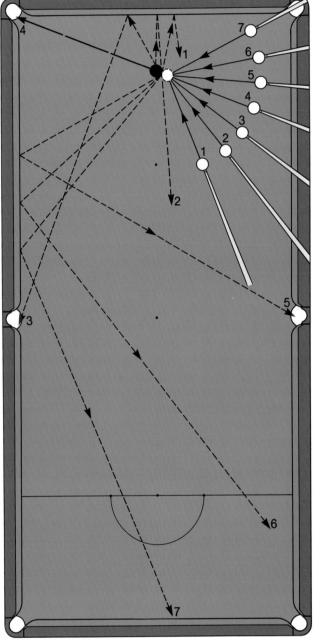

With the balls in the same position as before, try potting the blue into each of the top corner pockets, using the angles you have just practised on the previous exercise. Make a mental note of how far off the pocket you are and adjust the angle accordingly until you are able to pot the blue.

This exercise provides very good practice for learning the potting angles and will come in very useful during a game, since you should always try to play around the black spot where possible. Reading from 1 to 7, you need to set up the red balls for a quarter, half, threequarter and full-ball pot both below and above the black. The broken lines indicate the path the cue ball will take after contact with the black when playing a plain-ball shot. You should try to remember where the cue ball runs, since this will be important for positional play on the next red, after you have potted the black.

INTRODUCTION

BY STEVE DAVIS

When you watch professional players, either on television or live during a tournament, some of them can make the game look difficult and at times laborious. When they are faced with certain types of shot, there seems to be a major problem to overcome. In contrast other players are so fluent round the table that they make the game look so easy as to be ridiculous, considering how hard it really is to play that well.

Jimmy White is probably the one player in the game at the moment who inspires more young people to start playing than any other professional. This is not just because of his style and approach. He makes snooker look so easy that everyone watching thinks they've got a chance to do it as well.

One of Jimmy's greatest assets, which to an extent all good professionals have, but not always to the same degree, is his amazing ability to work out a shot quickly. His brain seems to tell him instinctively and instantly what type of shot to play in any given situation. This not only involves the pot itself, but what he wants to do with the cue ball afterwards – and that's all about ball control.

Almost in a split second – the time it takes Jimmy to walk round the table and get down to play the next shot – he has already made up his mind and knows exactly how he is going to play, what ball to go for and what type of spin he is going to put on the cue ball. In a way, he is at one with the table, almost part of the table, so close to the table that he understands what the balls are going to do instinctively.

You could draw parallels with the past craze for Space Invader machines, where the most expert players seemed so much aware of the machine and what was going on that they might have been joined to it.

Jimmy is the ultimate of all the professionals in this respect. The only problem for anyone trying to study or copy him is that it is very difficult to break his style of play down and analyse it. It is really a case of natural ability taken to its limits. Jimmy would be the first to admit that he's never had to study or work on technique to the extent that others must, because he's been blessed with a very strong technique anyway – a natural style.

Although everyone should strive to master the kind of ball control that Jimmy so wonderfully demonstrates, I would add that his approach to the game is not the ideal one to follow until you have mastered properly all the basic techniques in the earlier part of the book. You certainly need to have a very thorough grounding in the essentials of the game before you can even consider playing in a similar style. The main danger of trying to mimic his approach is not in the range of shots he plays but the speed at which he plays them. If as a young amateur you try to play as quickly, you will soon come unstuck, because at the early stages you will need more time to think about what you are doing. Before you play a shot, you must have assessed the situation carefully and gone through all the possibilities – and everyone does this at a different speed.

Where you come across players with a similar style and approach to Jimmy, you will find that they have an abundance of natural ability, an uncanny instinct for the game. To be quite honest, they are also probably not the sort of people who will spend hours studying a book such as this, except to check on the basic elements of technique. They tend to be copy players, who have developed their game by watching their heroes closely. Jimmy's idol in the Seventies was Alex Higgins. He copied certain aspects of the Hurricane's game and created his own style within that. A similar thing has happened with the exciting young Scotsman Stephen Hendry, whose idol was Jimmy himself. Doubtless in years to come youngsters will copy Stephen.

What you must remember, however, is that all these players built up their own game on sound basic techniques that provided the groundwork for their own skills. As you progress through to this section of the book and look at the more complex techniques of ball control – using spin, awkward bridging and planning shots, you will be relying on those elementary aspects of the game without which you can never hope to reach the level of play and consistency of a Jimmy White, Tony Meo or Willie Thorne – or any of the top professionals, for that matter.

When it comes to controlling the cue ball, an essential part of competitive snooker in putting together frame-winning breaks, Jimmy has a phenomenal repertoire of shots. There is so much he can do with the cue ball – from a gentle touch to a full-blooded power shot, that at times I wonder how he makes up his mind what type of shot to play.

Of course this range of ability is not something that every player possesses. Other people find there is a limit to their cueing power or their ability to put side on the ball. They are therefore restricted to what kind of shots they can play in any given situation and may find that in some cases they have only one choice.

Developing a wide a range of shots is obviously of enormous benefit to any player. Depending on what you can do with the cue ball, you open up many more options as to how to get on to the next ball – or which ball to get on to. This is very important when you come on to positional play, which is discussed later. This part of the game is all about control of the cue ball – and that doesn't simply mean power. You have to know exactly what the cue ball is doing – or can do – and in this section Jimmy explains how you can impose this type of control and what effects it has.

When you watch a top game of snooker, it seems as though the cue ball just glides over the cloth. But it is rare for it simply to be rolling in any direction. Usually it is carrying some element of spin that controls where it ends up.

BALL CONTROL

BY JIMMY WHITE

The game of snooker is all about control – in the stance, in the preparation for a shot and in the playing of that shot. The earlier sections of this book have concentrated on those basic techniques, without which you cannot possibly tackle any of the more advanced aspects of the game.

Once you can take up the correct position at the table, line up for the shot, perfect your cueing technique, strike the ball in a dead straight line and take on a pot at whatever angle, then you can consider those ways in which you can control the cue ball after it has made contact with the object ball.

This is crucial if you want to become a more consistent and fluent competitor, since it enables you to guarantee position on the next shot and therefore build up a break – hopefully to put you in a match-winning situation. But the control required to determine the direction of the cue ball depends primarily on two aspects of the strike. Firstly, you must be able to hit the cue ball in exactly the right spot and, secondly, you must play that shot with the correct amount of pace.

It is hard enough to achieve one of these objectives. That is why it is absolutely critical that you have perfected the basic techniques before you attempt to use advanced shots, which all involve spin on the ball and pin-point accuracy in the strike.

UNDERSTANDING SPIN

Before I explain about the different types of spin, when you should use them and what effect they have, it is important to understand the principle of putting spin on the cue ball. If you cannot take in how this affects the run of the cue ball then you will gain no advantage from using it and will, as a consequence, restrict yourself to low-scoring breaks and therefore deny yourself the opportunity to break through into top competitive snooker.

Initially there are two types of spin that you should concentrate on – back spin and top spin. The other option is side spin, which I will discuss later in this section.

With both back and top spin you must be aiming through the centre of the cue ball. You need to imagine a line running from top to bottom down the middle of the ball and aim to strike it either above or below centre. For top spin you will need to aim the tip of your cue towards the top of the ball, while for back spin your cue tip should strike below the centre. Depending on how much spin you want to put on the ball, you will need to aim higher or lower towards the extreme edge.

It is not easy to imagine the effect these types of spin have on the cue ball without playing them. But in very simple terms, if you play top spin on the cue ball you are enabling it to accelerate forward after contact with the object ball, when it has maximum grip on the cloth. The spin is forward, as the motion of the ball.

With back spin, the effect is totally the reverse. What you are imparting on the cue ball is a backward spin, so that once it strikes the object ball, the effect of the spin after gripping the cloth is such that the cue ball rolls back the way it came.

Obviously there are other factors that control the effect of the spin. The most important of these is the distance between the cue ball and the object ball.

This illustration should help you understand what happens to the cue ball when you apply either top or back spin. In contrast to a plain-ball shot, where you strike the cue ball dead centre, with top spin you need to make contact above the centre. The effect is to send the cue ball forward in the normal way but when it makes contact with the object ball it gains momentum with the forward spin and carries on. With back spin, you strike the cue ball below the centre, Again it travels forward normally until making contact with the object ball. Then the effect is reversed and the cue ball will move back towards you with the spin.

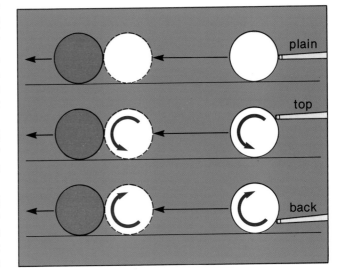

This is quite logical if you think about it, since the longer the cue ball is in contact with the cloth, the more the cloth is likely to affect its movement forward. This is why, when playing the back spin, you can achieve three quite different effects – screw, stun and drag – depending on how far the cue ball has to travel.

Before I explain about these, there is an exercise that Terry recommends which highlights the range of effects you can get from imparting either top or back spin to the cue ball.

Place the pink ball on its spot and the cue ball midway between it and one of the centre pockets, so that the balls are in a straight line between that pocket and the opposite top corner pocket.

First play a plain-ball shot to pot the pink with medium pace and full follow-through. You will find the cue ball will also run through into the same pocket. Now respot the balls and play the same shot, but this time with maximum top spin, aiming the cue tip top centre of the cue ball. If hit correctly, the cue ball will follow the pink into the pocket, but much more quickly.

Now play the same pot, but this time apply maximum back spin, striking the cue ball bottom centre, and only follow-through about half the normal distance. The cue ball will spin back into the centre pocket, the speed at which it travels depending on the pace of the cue when the cue ball leaves the tip in the follow-through.

This illustrates well the basic effect of applying either top or back spin to the cue ball, depending on where you strike it and the power and timing of the shot.

APPLYING BACK SPIN

As I have already explained, to put back spin on the cue ball you have to hit it bottom centre. To ensure the success of this shot, you must aim low enough on the cue ball, play the shot with sufficient pace and shorten your follow-through.

In order to play the cue ball near the bottom, you will have to lower your bridge to ensure the cue still moves on a plane parallel to the table. To do this, you will have to flatten your fingers and lower your thumb, using your forefinger more to help guide the cue. You may find you have to turn your hand

slightly, raising the outside to push the inside down nearer the cloth.

This highlights one of the most common problems when playing back spin – lifting the butt of the cue and aiming down to the bottom of the ball. If you do this, you not only limit any follow-through, but you are in danger of mis-cueing and making the ball bounce, which will obviously alter the final effect of the spin.

Another tendency is to snatch at the shot, raising the cue on the follow-through and lifting the head up. You must keep a smooth fluent action right through the shot, making sure you remain absolutely still with your head well down over the cue. The success of any back spin shot is dependent on these aspects, as it is on the power of your cueing action and the timing.

SCREW

When you apply back spin and the cue ball runs back towards you after making contact with the object ball, it is a screw shot. How far back you can bring it will depend on how far it has to run over the cloth before hitting the object ball, how much spin you apply and the amount of power you put into the stroke.

Because the ball comes back towards you, when you first start playing this shot there is a great tendency to snatch your cue away too soon for fear the ball will hit it. But the fact is you will always have that split second to hold your position at the stop to ensure you do not move too early. The consequences of this I have already discussed.

Bear in mind that it is easier to screw back a short distance. Because the further the cue ball travels the more the cloth dissipates the back spin, the more power you have to use to retain the spin. So you not only have to make sure you have hit the cue ball in exactly the right place, but you have to play it that

To apply back spin you need to strike the cue ball below the centre. The common tendency is to lift the butt end of the cue, but you must keep the cue parallel. This means lowering your bridge. As you can see here, my hand is virtually flat on the table to ensure the cue comes through as low as possible to make the right contact for the shot.

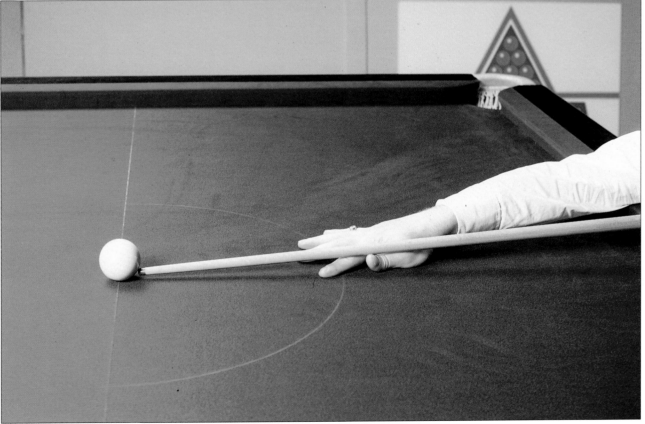

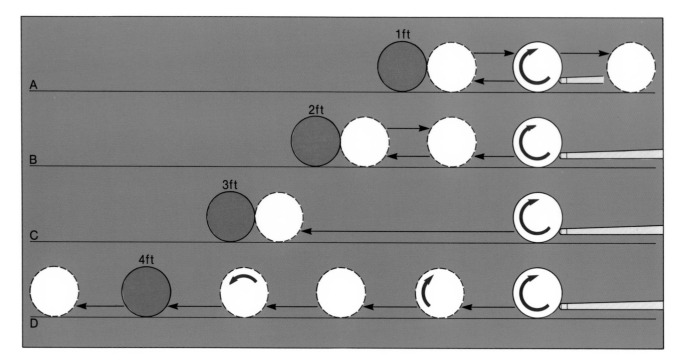

Here you can see the different effects possible by playing with back spin, depending on the distance the cue ball has to travel to the object ball. In each case the shot is played at the same pace. With example A, because of the short distance the cue ball has to travel, it is very easy to screw back behind the original position. By increasing the distance in example B, the cue ball will screw back, but not so far. With example C, the extra distance means that the cue ball will stop on contact with the object ball as the effect of the spin wears off. This is a stun shot. The further the cue ball has to travel to the object ball, the more the effect changes, so that with example D the back spin actually wears off and eventually the cue ball will roll forward. This is the drag shot.

much stronger, which makes the possibility of mistakes more likely.

I believe the screw shot is a very important part of the game. Equally, my advice to the beginner is to leave it alone completely until you have really mastered hitting the cue ball dead centre. If you can use it successfully, you get tremendous control over the cue ball and will find it an ideal way of getting out of trouble in tight situations.

I cannot stress enough the importance of timing for this shot, as well as keeping absolutely still, with your head well down, and ensuring the cue goes through the ball on the hit. This is therefore a very hard shot to play accurately and well and a lot of players cannot do it.

STUN

The stun shot is also played with back spin, but the basic difference between this and the screw is that there is no follow-through. You should aim to strike the cue ball just below the centre and stop the cue after impact. Naturally you will be restricting the pace of the ball and therefore the effect of the back spin will wear off as it travels along the cloth, stopping dead on impact with the object ball.

The main advantage of using stun is that you can keep more control over the cue ball and guarantee where it will stop, which makes it very useful for positional play.

Personally I would recommend you learn this shot before attempting to screw back. It involves less power and more 'feel'. In playing it you will have greater control over the cue ball and, having mastered the principle of striking just below centre, you can then work your way down to a full screw shot position.

The main danger of this shot is when going for a

pot, since if you miss it you have denied yourself any safety route away and you will almost certainly have let your opponent in. You should therefore not attempt it unless you have a relatively easy pot and are confident of getting it.

I recall one occasion in particular where the stun shot came to my rescue. I was playing against Cliff Thorburn in the 1986 Mercantile Credit Classic which, incidentally, I went on to win. Cliff had snookered me and I was forced to play off two cushions to get at the pink. The problem was that I was likely to get a double kiss on the cue ball, which could have been disastrous.

I decided to stun the shot so that the cue ball would still travel through but slowly enough to avoid the double kiss. I played the shot to perfection and, as luck would have it, the pink ended up behind the black to give me a snooker, from which I won the frame.

STUN RUN-THROUGH

This is one of the most useful shots in the game, since it not only gives you greater control over the cue ball but also enables you to gain a range of positions for the next shot. The stun run-through comes between the stun and the top spin shot and its effect will depend on where exactly you strike the cue ball and how much power you use.

Normally you would aim just above centre on the cue ball, but lower than for top spin. You can still play this shot by striking below centre, but in this case you need a much softer touch to create the same effect. And because the touch on the ball is crucial for determining how it will respond, you will have to spend a lot of time experimenting on the different effects and positions you can gain. Again, you can use the exercise with the pink ball on its spot to see how stun run-through works.

The great advantage of this type of shot is highlighted when you are potting at an angle, since the range of positions you can gain from it are almost limitless.

DRAG

One of the problems with a long shot, particularly when you want to make a softish contact with the object ball, is retaining sufficient control over the cue ball and ensuring it does not run off course through the effect of the nap of the cloth. This is a particular danger when you play the cue ball more slowly.

If you put back spin on the ball, you can immediately strike it that much more firmly, which will overcome any effect from the nap. The pace at which it strikes the object ball and the distance it runs on after contact will depend on how far away the cue ball is to the object ball. The principle involves using the back spin to slow the ball down, so that in effect the spin wears off just before it reaches the object ball and runs forward at the desired pace. This obviously requires good judgement of both distance and power in the shot and is something you will need to practise a lot to be able to gauge it accurately.

A typical situation in which you are likely to use this shot is when playing a long red over the pocket and you want to stay on the black or possibly the pink. If you use drag, when the cue ball has struck the object ball it will run on to the cushion and stop so that you can hold good position for your next shot.

APPLYING TOP SPIN

As I mentioned earlier, to apply top spin to the cue ball you need to strike it above the centre – and the higher up you make contact the more top spin you will put on it. In effect you are making the ball spin forward faster than it is travelling, so that you can maintain the pace after contact with the object ball. This is particularly useful when you are playing a thick contact with the object ball, which necessarily would offer greater resistance to the cue ball.

To play with top spin, you must make sure your cue is coming through parallel but higher up on the cue ball. To achieve this, you must lift your bridge by arching the hand more, bringing your fingers in slightly. This will weaken your bridge a fraction and you must take this into consideration when playing the shot. The more power you use, the greater the chance of movement – and therefore not striking the cue ball in exactly the right position.

Further pressure is put on the bridge because with top spin you need a full follow-through with the cue after the hit. So control here is very important.

I personally believe everyone should try to be a

good top spin player. You will find it is much easier to pot balls successfully using this spin – more so than with screw, stun or side.

There is an interesting shot you can try using top spin when you have mastered the technique. We call it a 'banana shot'. Put a ball over the pocket and place the cue ball in the 'D'. If you strike with extreme top, it has got so much spin on that when it hits the cushion after contact with the object ball it bounces and stops. So, in effect, it is like playing a screw shot but you are using the cushion to reverse the cue ball.

APPLYING SIDE

It is unbelievable at times what side can do to the cue ball. But before you get carried away with the thought, I must stress that it is one of the hardest shots in the game to play consistently and well – and, most importantly, with control. So my advice is not to rush in until you are competent to strike any part of the cue ball accurately.

Obviously side can be a very useful shot to play and, because of the range of positions you can get off the cushion, it is an essential part of large break-building. Having said that, I don't believe you need to play this type of shot until you have reached at least the '30' break stage.

To appreciate how difficult a shot it is to play effectively, you should consider the other forms of spin I have just talked about. In every case so far, the shots involve centre line contact, albeit above or below the middle of the cue ball. With side, you have to adjust your aim to hit the edge of the ball, either on the left or the right.

What you must get firmly fixed in your mind is that you are still aiming to play the cue ball in a straight line to the object ball. There is a great tendency to push the cue ball deliberately in the opposite direction to that of the side – that is, if you are playing with left-hand side and striking on the left of the cue ball,

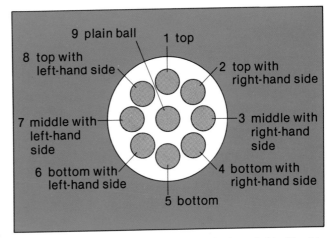

This illustration shows clearly where on the cue ball you need to strike to effect the different types of spin and side. Use this as a basic guide, but obviously make adjustments as required.

you want to push the ball out to the right. Having pushed the cue ball off line, the effect of the spin will bring it back again through the nap of the cloth, but not necessarily at the right time to make the contact you want with the object ball.

Already you can see for yourself how great the margins for error are with this type of shot.

The basic reason for using side is, as I have said, to increase the range of positions you can achieve off the object ball. As the cue ball strikes the cushion after contact with the object ball, it will come off at different angles to a plain-ball shot. Depending on the type of side and how much you apply, you can vary these angles. But you will have to experiment with this to see exactly what happens and then remember the different effects you can achieve with side.

One exercise I used to find very helpful was to play a straight blue off its spot into one of the top corner pockets. First of all play the pot using top spin, with the cue ball following through. Then use bottom and screw the cue ball back. Now try the same shot but apply side. To begin with, you will be surprised by how much you miss the shot.

The effect of side is probably best illustrated by experimenting with the straight hitting exercise playing the cue ball off the brown spot up the table. Watch how the cue ball reacts off the top cushion

To apply top spin to the cue ball you need to strike it above the centre. Again, it is most important that you keep your cue as parallel as possible and do not drop the butt end. To achieve this, you have to raise your bridge by bringing the fingers in slightly and arching the hand, as you can see here. Bear in mind, however, that this will weaken your bridge a little.

when you apply different amounts of left and right-hand side.

To use side intelligently and effectively you must first understand the principle of what happens to the cue ball. Then you must learn how this affects the run of the ball after contact with the object ball and the angle at which it comes off the cushion. Finally you must try to remember all this. And if you consider this in relation to a straight pot, just imagine the additional variation on position you can gain from potting at an angle!

The one time that players usually use side is when breaking off at the start of a frame, since this makes it much easier to bring the cue ball round the top and side cushions and back into baulk. This shot you should certainly practise, but at least it is made easier by the fact that the balls are always in the same position on the table at this stage and any slight error in the shot should not make too much difference.

My final word must be one of caution. Although you will get those players who use side a lot – and Willie, in fact, plays every shot with a trace of it – only use it when you are confident and experienced enough to be able to control it. And unless you feel you are in Willie's class, don't use it unless you have to.

And when you do play with side – or use any other type of spin, for that matter – remember that it is vital to remain absolutely still in the shot. The slightest movement will destroy it. Have a good look at the shot first and make up your mind how you are going to play it. If you are not sure about exactly how to play it once you are down, then get up from the table and start again. Any late adjustment at the table, which I find is most common when people are playing with side, can be fatal.

This sequence gives you a player's view of where on the cue ball the cue tip should make contact for each of the basic types of spin and side. Depending on the effect you require, these will necessarily have to be adjusted. The shots shown (left to right from the top) are: top, top with right-hand side, right-hand side, bottom with right-hand side, bottom (or back spin), bottom with left-hand side, left-hand side, top with left-hand side and finally centre (or plain-ball).

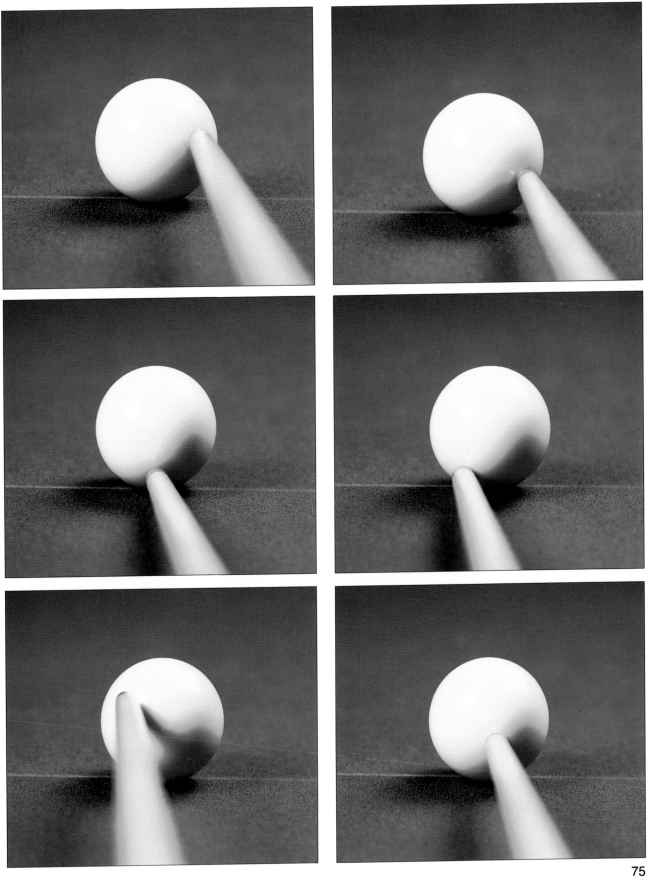

The line-up is a useful way of practising not only the potting angles but also control of the cue ball. There are different ways of setting it up, but the standard one is to position the reds between the black, pink and blue, with two reds below the blue. You can make the exercise harder by putting two reds between the black and the top cushion. The exercise involves potting a red and then a colour until you have cleared all the balls.

PRACTICE

PLAYING THE LINE-UP

This is a very popular exercise which you can play in a variety of ways. It is valuable because it brings in most of the shots you will need to play and, at the same time, helps you get used to all the angles.

To set the line-up, put the colours on their spots and then position the reds between the black and blue in a straight line up the centre of the table. Normally you would put 13 reds between the black and the blue, with the last two reds just below the blue. You can make it harder by putting two reds between the top cushion and the black.

The basic exercise is to pot a red, then a colour, then a red again until you have cleared the balls. Obviously this takes a lot of practising.

It is also a useful exercise for practising control on the cue ball and positional play and I use it a lot when I am having problems with this. To make it more interesting, try playing it without the cue ball touching the cushion. If you can score 100 this way, you are doing very well.

Further variations on this exercise include potting the reds in order, starting from the top cushion and working back, and nominating beforehand which red you are going to get on to.

If you find, after a while, that this becomes a bit monotonous, you can make the situation more realistic and interesting by putting all the colours on their spots and then spreading the reds round the table, as Terry does. Make sure the majority are around the pink and black, since this is where you are likely to make the big breaks. Put a couple of reds behind the baulk line, then another couple between the baulk line and the blue spot and several between that and the pink spot to give you some pots into the centre pockets.

Make sure you leave the pink and black clear so you can pot these into the two top and centre pockets.

If you miss any particular shot, then try setting it up as closely as you can and play it again before continuing.

Terry uses this exercise a lot because it gives you all the variety you need for practising both the basics and more advanced shots.

Although it is more for the advanced player, there is no reason why beginners shouldn't try it too. The problem when you first start playing snooker is that you don't get the chance on the table to play enough shots. This way you can set the cue ball up where you want to give yourself easy shots and then progress to more difficult angles. The other advantage here is that you do not have to worry about safety play, but just concentrate on potting the balls.

POTTING THE COLOURS

This is one exercise that everyone should practise, since it is a situation that often occurs at the end of a frame and one you should always take advantage of because the position of the colours on their spots is always the same.

Set the colours up on their spots and then play to pot them in the right sequence – yellow through to black. And when you are potting the black, try to get the cue ball back down the table for position on the yellow. Having respotted the colours you can start again. See how many times you can keep this going.

What I then do is pot all the colours in sequence, set them all up again and try to pot them in reverse order starting from where the cue ball ended up on the black pot. You can keep this going, backwards and forwards through the colours for some time, although it's not as easy as it looks.

PRACTICE
MEASURING THE SCREW-BACK

An interesting exercise to see how far you can screw back the cue ball is to put a red close to the side cushion near one of the top pockets, with the cue ball about 2 in away. Keep playing the screw shot and try to judge how far back you can bring the cue ball.

Neal and I can screw the cue ball right back to the baulk cushion. If you can do this, then you are hitting the ball very well indeed.

Another way of seeing the effect of back spin and how well you can control the distance you bring the ball back is by trying an exercise that Steve uses. Put the blue ball on its spot and the cue ball about a foot away towards one of the middle pockets.

First practise hitting the blue ball so the object ball stops dead. Then try bringing the cue ball back just a few inches, then 1 ft, then 18 in. and then 2 ft. You can set marker balls alongside and aim to get the cue ball back to each of those in turn. Finally try screwing back so the cue ball stops on the very edge of the middle pocket.

This is an excellent way of learning how to control the amount of back spin you put on the cue ball and how to judge the pace of the shot for final position.

One problem here is that screwing back does take its toll on the tip of your cue, particularly if you practise these shots for any length of time. You will find after a couple of hours you have probably lost one side of the tip.

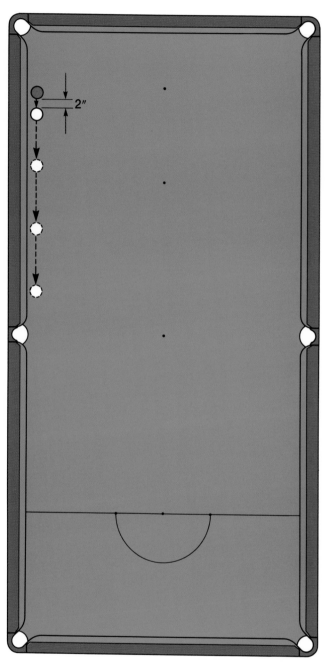

One way of measuring how far you can screw back the cue ball is to put a red near the cushion with the cue ball about 2 in away. Practise bringing the cue ball back a little further each time.

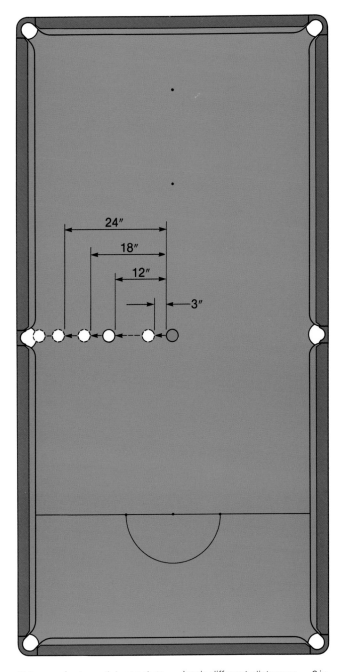

24"

18"

12"

3"

PRACTICE

PLAYING OFF CUSHIONS WITH SIDE

An interesting exercise that will help you judge the effect of side on the cue ball is to play it off the side cushions (overleaf) and see where it goes. Try it using both left and right-hand side and watch the path of the cue ball after it hits the cushion. This can be a very effective way of getting out of a snooker, if you can judge the spin right.

You will find this quite difficult to start with, because you have to know how much side you are putting on the cue ball and also judge the difference in pace. It is all a question of feel and touch.

Another exercise that will help you judge the effect of side is playing the cue ball down the middle of the table over the spots, using both left and right-hand side, and trying to bring the cue ball off the top cushion and into the centre and then the bottom pockets.

This is a particularly tough exercise, which you should not expect to achieve very often. But it will certainly help you judge how much side to put on the cue ball for the different angles.

This exercise is useful not only to see the effect of back spin but also to learn how to control it. Put the blue ball on its spot and the cue ball about 12 in away in line with one of the middle pockets. Then try screwing the cue ball back different distances – 3 in, 12 in, 18 in and 24 in. Finally try bringing it back to the edge of the pocket. You can use marker balls to give you the exact target to aim for.

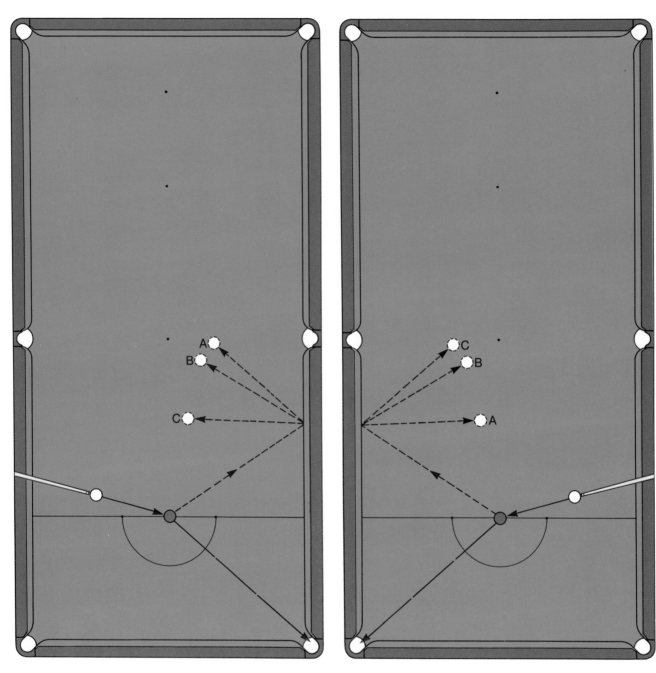

A useful set of exercises is to see the effect of side on the cue ball when playing off a cushion. Here I have set up a half-ball pot on the brown from its spot. You can see clearly the different direction of the cue ball off the cushion between a shot with left-hand side (A), a plain-ball shot (B) and one with right-hand side (C). If you play the same shots but from the other side of the table the situations are reversed. There are of course many variations, but at least you will learn to understand how the cushion effects shots with side.

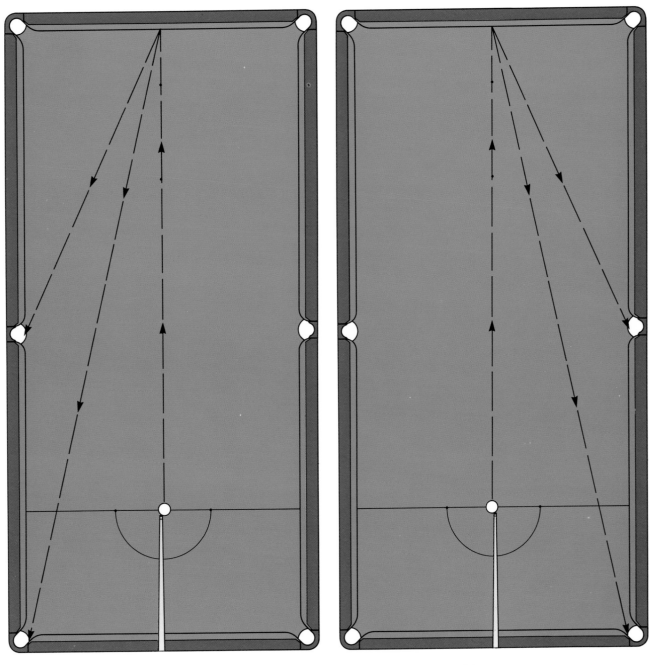

This exercise will also show the effect of side when playing off a cushion. With the cue ball on the brown spot, play it up the spots using first left-hand side and then right-hand side. Having made a note of what happens to the cue ball, try potting it off the top cushion, first into the centre pocket, then the bottom pocket on both sides of the table. You need to use left-hand side for the left of the table and right-hand side for the right.

VARIATIONS ON CUEING
INTRODUCTION BY STEVE DAVIS

There is no doubt that Tony Meo is one of the best players never to have won a major ranking tournament and proof of the overall quality and standard of the professional game. No one is a better judge of how good Tony is as a player than myself, since it is no coincidence that as partners we have done so well in the world doubles championships over the last few years, winning the title four times. I am pleased he is my partner, as no doubt he is that I am his.

I grew up with Tony through the amateur ranks and as far as my apprenticeship in and around London is concerned, Tony was always my main adversary. So I have known Tony for a long time both as a competitor and a friend, particularly since he joined me as the second member of the Matchroom team.

Tony is a great player and has got every shot in the book. I am sure that he only needs one good season of results to prove to others what I already know and get the recognition he deserves.

As the shortest of the Matchroom players, it doesn't take any great brain to work out that Tony tends to use the rest more often than taller players with more reach when he finds himself out of position. To this extent he is the perfect example of a player who has no fear of using the extra equipment on the table. And there are times when we all have to use one of the rests or cope with awkward bridging.

When you reach the level of play that comes with professional status, the whole idea of the game is to keep the cue ball in positions that are free from any obstacles or hindrances, such as playing over other balls or where you cannot put your bridging hand firmly on the table. This only comes with experience and skill at controlling the cue ball. And, even then, sometimes we still have to play from such a position.

But part of the apprenticeship you go through as an amateur or inexperienced player is that you often find yourself in an awkward position because you have not mastered total control over the cue ball – or, of course, your opponent has put you in an awkward position on the table. The value of this section is that you should be able to feel comfortable to play any type of shot, with or without the equipment available, and should never shy away from using what is necessary to play a difficult shot.

I have often seen players in a club climb on to the table rather than use the rest. You should never do this. Not only does it do the table no good, but it means you never give yourself the chance of getting used to using those implements that sometimes offer you a far better chance of playing a particular shot more effectively.

Underneath every professsional tournament table there is a complete factory of implements of all shapes and sizes. All have been specially designed to do a particular job in coping with virtually every conceivable situation on the table. In this section Tony explains how to play with and without their help. Whereas you would always try to play with just a bridged hand, there are times when this is impossible and you need to use one of the rests available.

I have recently been introduced to a very useful implement, a plastic 'V' which slots on to the fork of the rest. Depending on how high you need to bridge for the shot, you can fix it on to the high or low 'X' and I find it an excellent substitute for the spider or when I have an awkward cueing position along the cushion.

Whether you are having to form a variation on the basic bridged hand or use one of the range of implements specially designed for different situations, make sure that you can cue as freely as possible and that the support is firm and rigid and does not wobble about. You will never be able to play a shot cleanly and accurately if there is the slightest movement in the bridge.

VARIATIONS ON CUEING

BY TONY MEO

AWKWARD BRIDGING

Normal bridging has already been discussed in Part I and it is true that all players form their bridge in very much the same way. Naturally there are minor variations. For example, I tend to spread my fingers about half an inch apart, whereas some players prefer a wider spread.

One point to bear in mind here is that being a left-handed player I use my right hand to bridge, as you will see from the illustrations. Of course most people are right-handed and would therefore use the left hand to bridge. But the principles and technique are the same either way.

Terry has already stressed the importance of a firm, solid bridge, which is vital to ensure a good cue action, since you must form it in such a way as to maximise control as you take the cue back and bring it forward for the shot.

The same principles apply wherever you have to bridge on the table, since sometimes you will find the cue ball is close to or tight up against the cushion or possibly very near another ball. In such situations you will have to adopt a different bridge to suit. But you must still make sure the bridge you form is both comfortable and firm to give you the best chance of making the shot.

BRIDGING OVER THE CUSHION

No one likes playing the cue ball off the cushion and during a break you would normally avoid leaving yourself in this situation. If you do end up

The nearer the cue ball is to the cushion the more awkward bridging becomes. You can see here how my hand is pressed up against the cushion, but I am still able to form a conventional bridge with my thumb cocked and my fingers spread on the cloth. This is the nearest the cue ball can be to the cushion where I can do this.

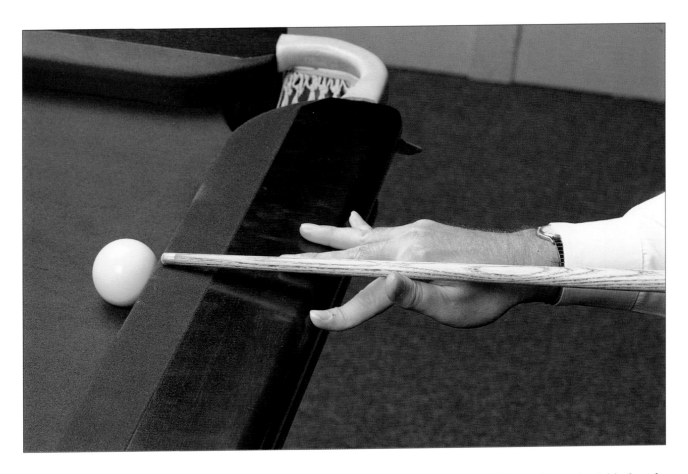

Above left: With the cue ball nearer the cushion, I have to bridge over it. In this position I like to use a looped bridge, with my thumb using the back edge of the table as a support. Although you are necessarily bridging that bit higher, you can keep the hand quite firm and avoid any movement.

Left: With the cue ball closer still, I have to bring my hand back further. It is still possible to keep the hand fairly rigid in this position, since I can create a 'V' with my thumb for the cue while supporting the bridge with the bottom of the hand pressed against the back edge of the table.

Above: This is obviously the weakest form of bridge, since only my fingers are in contact with the table. In this situation it is important to spread the fingers as wide as possible to help the stability. I can still form a reasonable 'V' for the cue, but because of the overall weakness I would not normally attempt anything more than a medium pace shot from here.

with the cue ball close to or touching the cushion, you have played a poor shot. Because this position naturally restricts the type of shot you can play, your opponent will often try to leave the cue ball as close to the cushion as possible at the end of his break.

There are two basic problems to overcome with this type of shot. The first is to form the best possible bridge, bearing in mind that you cannot place your hand flat on the table. You will see from the illustrations how I bridge over the cushion, depending on how close the cue ball is to the edge of the table. You will have to experiment on what suits you best, although the basic principles still apply – the bridge must be firm and solid.

The second problem is that you will not have a full ball to strike, which means you cannot hit it dead centre. And the closer it is to the cushion, the less area you will have for striking. This obviously restricts the type of shot you can play.

I find that if I shorten my cue grip, by bringing my hand forward, the shot feels more solid. Of course this does automatically restrict the cue action and you therefore have to be less ambitious with the type of shot you can play. But you will find that a degree of restraint in this situation will normally pay off.

The rule here is: when in doubt, play safe. Your prime objective is to concentrate on striking the cue

ball cleanly, since you don't want to mis-cue and possibly end up playing a foul shot.

As I said, nobody likes playing off the cushion, since it limits the control you have over the cue ball. Some players obviously cope better in this situation than others. Steve is probably the best under these circumstances and that is really down to his cue action. The better your cue action, the more chance you have of hitting the ball in the centre.

BRIDGING DOWN THE CUSHION

Another awkward shot is playing down the cushion. Trying to bridge successfully in this situation is made more difficult because often you find that half your hand is over the cushion and half off it.

Normally in this position I tend to use the loop bridge to give the cue more control in the shot. Naturally you must use what cushion you have to make your bridging hand as firm as possible and then

You will find players have different ways of bridging along the cushion. Personally I prefer using the looped bridge, since this gives me better control over the cue. You will see that my hand is providing good support on the cushion. Whatever you do, don't let the hand drop over the cushion.

form a loop with your forefinger through which to run the cue.

There are obviously variations and different players will tackle this in different ways. I find it works well for me and I notice that Willie tends to use it occasionally, as well. An alternative here is to rest part of your hand on the cushion and then drop your thumb down to form a tunnel.

This ensures a firm, level bridge. What you must avoid at all costs is letting your hand drop down over the side of the cushion since it then becomes impossible to strike the cue ball in the centre.

You can see more easily how the looped bridge works by looking at the illustration.

Bridging over a pocket is particularly awkward since there is so little on which to support your hand. I normally use the first two fingers and thumb to grip round the edge of the pocket, with the other two fingers resting on the edge of the table. I am still able to raise the thumb enough to form a 'V'.

BRIDGING OVER A POCKET

You will find that occasionally you have to bridge over a pocket. This is never easy because you have so little of the table to grip and therefore have to adapt your bridge as best you can. The only contact, as you can see from the illustration, is with your fingers, since there is nowhere to rest your hand.

The important thing, as with all awkward bridging, is to take your time and make sure you are comfortable. Never just get down and play the shot because you will rarely hit the cue ball cleanly this way. Your bridging arm will naturally take a lot more of the control here and you should only play the shot when

you feel nice and steady and have a straight, firm cueing action.

Feeling right for the shot is absolutely vital and here Steve is the best example to follow. If he has a problem or does not feel comfortable with a shot, he will take time to settle down and will only play it when everything is right.

BRIDGING OVER A BALL

This is certainly to my mind the hardest shot to play, particularly when, like me, your reach is limited. There is no doubt that taller players have a distinct advantage in this situation since they can get over the ball more easily and that added height on the shot can make all the difference. Having long fingers is an added bonus, since these enable them to clear the ball in the way more comfortably.

As with all bridging situations, you need to get your hand settled as firmly as possible on the table,

even though the only contact is through the tips of your fingers. Because you will be putting quite a lot of strain on them, you will not be able to hold this bridge for any length of time. It is therefore important to have worked out exactly the shot you want to play and where you can comfortably position your bridging hand before you get down for the shot.

If you watch carefully, you will see players trying out positions for their fingers first and this is particularly necessary when you are having to bridge into the pack of reds, for example. In this situation there is no clear area of table and you have to work out where to place each finger without touching or disturbing any

Above and right: Bridging over a ball is always tricky, since in this position you only have the tips of your fingers with which to grip the table and provide adequate support. The more you can spread these, the firmer your bridge will be. Again players will adopt different bridges here. What is important is that it is as rigid and comfortable as possible.

of the surrounding balls. If you do, that is of course a foul shot.

You can best see how to bridge in these circumstances by looking at the illustration, although every situation will be slightly different and you will just

have to experiment on what is the firmest, most comfortable position at the time. When in doubt, you must get up from the shot, settle yourself and then start again. And remember, the longer you wait on the shot, the weaker your bridge will become.

If you really do not feel happy with your bridge and the shot you have to play, then you may well have to resort to using the spider, which I will discuss in a minute.

The golden rule is to make sure you hit the cue ball cleanly. You may well be in a position to take on a pot from here but you will have to weigh up the averages since normally you will do well to achieve the pot, let alone gain position for the next shot.

When I am faced with a particularly awkward position, I am pleased with simply hitting the ball cleanly and not playing a foul shot. If the object ball goes in, then really that is a bonus. In the end, it is all down to percentages and, of course, the state of the game at the time. You may decide that it is best to play safe and just trickle the cue ball up to the object ball.

No player enjoys this type of shot, but as I said earlier the taller you are the greater the advantage. That is why people like Steve and Willie are better equipped to cope with it and not make a mistake.

Above and right: Probably the hardest type of bridge is when you are playing the cue ball from within a cluster of other balls. Often it is impossible to use the equipment, such as the spider or swan-neck,

and you simply have to experiment on the firmest and most comfortable position, depending on how the balls lie. Again, try and spread the fingers as wide as you can within the space available.

A further variation on bridging is when you have to get on the table to play a shot. Although you can still use the conventional bridging approach, you must make sure that your body is still and that you can move the cue freely. And don't forget – one foot on the floor, otherwise it's a foul stroke.

PLAYING OVER THE TABLE

Although this is not strictly a matter of having to bridge awkwardly, because you are resting most of your body over the table and only standing on one leg, the same principles of balance and comfort still apply.

It is impossible to offer specific guidance here, since every situation will be slightly different. The rules state that there has to be one point of contact with the floor, even though this may be just the tip of your shoe.

If you do decide to 'get on the table', you must make sure that you do not touch any of the balls with your body and, obviously, that you are not over-stretching or restricting your cue action. Other than that, you simply have to find the most comfortable position for playing the shot.

As a general rule, you should explore every possible way of playing a shot without having to use a rest. But naturally there are limits to the positions from which you can reasonably play a shot and you should not be frightened of using this equipment if you are not happy with the shot otherwise.

GETTING USED TO BRIDGING

There is really no advice I can give on practising awkward bridging. All I can suggest is that you set up different situations round the table and experiment with your bridging hand. The more you play, the more comfortable the bridge will feel and the more confident you will be in awkward situations.

The important thing is to remember the basic principles – to get the maximum contact you can with the table and then create as firm and stable a channel for your cue when striking the ball. Usually you will find that the most comfortable position naturally provides the best bridge.

USING THE REST

Naturally using the rest is never quite the same as playing with a bridged hand, but there are times when you will need it and you should therefore practise with it to build up your confidence. Having said that ideally you should never play yourself into a position where you have to use it, that is obviously

unrealistic. Equally, you may find yourself left with a shot from your opponent which requires using it.

You should not be afraid of the rest and it is certainly a mistake to over-reach for a shot rather than take the rest. Treat it as an extension of your bridge, which is basically all that it is.

Deciding when to use the rest will obviously depend on the position of the cue ball and the length of your reach. This is where the taller players have an advantage, since they can stretch further down the table. This is why Steve, Willie and Neal would normally play less shots with it than, say, Jimmy or myself. But everyone must know how to use it – and when to use it.

Where you position the rest on the table will depend on how the other balls are placed. But you should always hold it to one side so that it does not interfere with the line of the shot and your cueing action. You will notice that the rest has a high and low 'X'. Which one you use is basically a matter of personal preference. I play with the low 'X', as normally most of us do.

One school of thought maintains that you should use the high 'X' for striking the top half of the cue ball and the low 'X' for screw shots. But the low 'X' is closer to the normal height of your bridge and does ensure that you keep your cue as horizontal as possible.

The main difference for shots of this kind is in the way you hold your cue, which you would normally do from the side as you can see clearly from the illustration. Otherwise, you line up the shot in the normal way. You need to get your head down as low as possible in line with the shot; otherwise your cueing action is the same, apart from the sideways movement of the cueing arm. Make sure you keep this as level with the table as possible.

Just as you would with a normal shot, you must keep everything as still as possible and of course make sure that you are comfortable before you play the shot. You will probably find you need to widen your stance slightly to get down low enough.

Where most mistakes are made are in not striking the cue ball cleanly and accurately. After lining up the shot, I take my eye off the object ball and concentrate on that part of the cue ball I am aiming to hit.

Generally you will find you cannot be quite as

You may have noticed that I am playing right-handed with the rest although I am a left-handed player. Strangely I find this more natural and more comfortable. Where you place the rest on the table will depend on the position of other balls, but you should keep it to one side so that it doesn't interfere with the line of the shot or your cueing action. The grip is over the top of the cue, with your right arm pointing outwards and parallel to the table. Try and get as low down to the shot as possible.

With the arrival of the extension, long cueing has been made so much easier and more reliable. The half-butt was a very cumbersome instrument and it was impossible to get any 'feel' in the shot. Here, as you can see, you tend to be more upright in the shot and therefore should not attempt anything too ambitious.

ambitious with your shots when playing with the rest, although it is possible to achieve a fair degree of control over the cue ball. You will need to adjust the position of the 'X' slightly, depending on whether you want to hit top, centre or bottom of the cue ball. You should not dip or raise your cue for this, since this will upset your normal cueing action and probably result in a mis-hit.

One little idiosyncracy here is that although I am a left-handed player, I use the rest as if I was playing right-handed. I really cannot explain why I do this, except that it feels more natural this way and, most importantly, more comfortable. If for any reason you do find it particularly awkward using the rest one way, then why not try changing hands? You never know, it might work for you as well.

Most professional players use the rest very well, particularly Jimmy and Terry. Dennis, on the other hand, hates using the rest and you will often see him switching over and playing left-handed in order to reach the shot with it. Unfortunately not everyone is as ambidexterous as the Irishman!

USING AN EXTENSION

Before the introduction of the cue extension, the only option you had for long-reaching shots was the half-butt and long rest. The main problems, as I mentioned when I talked about equipment, were that you were not using your own cue and cue tip and the length of cue made it very unstable.

Fortunately there are relatively few situations where you need this length of reach on a shot, although again shorter players are at a distinct disadvantage over those with longer arms. When you are faced with having to use this equipment, you will certainly benefit from having an extension piece.

If you have to use the half-butt, then you should never attempt anything ambitious. Restrict yourself to plain ball shots and keep your cueing action as smooth as possible, aiming just to stroke the cue ball. Apart from the straightforward pot, you will normally be looking to play safe with this type of shot.

With the extension, you will find you have much more control over the cue. The feel you get is simply that of playing with an extended cue and you should, with practice, be able to control the cue ball much

better. But the mere distance makes the shot a cumbersome one and caution should be your guide.

USING THE SPIDER

This piece of equipment is only necessary when you cannot comfortably cue over other balls on to the cue ball. Obviously you should make sure that you cannot use the bridged hand for the shot. Normally the spider is only used where you would otherwise be over-reaching with this awkward bridge or where there is no room to form a bridge, usually when the cue ball is in among the pack of reds.

Although the principle is much the same as using the rest, you will necessarily be hitting down on to the cue ball and any real control is impossible. You should therefore concentrate on striking the cue ball as cleanly as possible and not attempt anything ambitious. It is the easiest thing in the world to miscue off this kind of shot.

Nobody enjoys using the spider, but there are occasionally times when you have no other choice – more so when your reach is restricted. So it is well worth practising using this piece of equipment. Not only can it get you out of trouble, but it can open up the game if you are attempting to pot a red out of the pack to leave yourself on the black.

THE MOVING FINGER

I could not end this section without making reference to my twitchy finger. I have often been asked about this and normally people express surprise that it does not affect my concentration. To be perfectly honest, I don't even notice it, although by now I am obviously aware that it happens.

Of course I have to put it down to nerves, but the important thing is that it doesn't affect the stability of my bridge, since the rest of my hand remains dead still.

The reason I mention this is that although you certainly want to avoid adopting such idiosyncracies, you should not let them put you off if they do develop. It is just one of those things that happens – and not just to me. Both John Virgo and Kirk Stevens do it, too!

The spider can be very useful where you are unable to cue comfortably over another ball, particularly where the shot is just out of reach. Care must be taken here since you are cueing from quite an upright position to get the height over the obstructing ball. Make sure you sight right down the cue and, again, don't try anything fancy.

PRACTICE

BRIDGING ON THE CUSHION

One way of getting used to awkward bridging and perfecting your potting at the same time is by practising an exercise that Steve uses. Put the cue ball against the bottom cushion in line with the brown spot and try hitting it straight into each of the two top pockets. Then you can try to do the same into the middle pockets, which you will find much harder.

USING THE RESTS

Because you need to get the feel of the rest and the spider, it is good practice to set up different situations on the table and try cueing with these. It is certainly worth spending some time on this, since you want to feel comfortable and confident should you find yourself in a position where you have to use them in a match.

PLANNING SHOTS

INTRODUCTION BY STEVE DAVIS

Willie Thorne is without doubt one of the best – and arguably *the* best – players when it comes to planning shots and building up large breaks on the table. Once he gets on the black, with the reds in the top half of the table, he is mustard. When he is playing well, you know he's got every chance of making a century break.

This skill, which to a greater or lesser extent all professional players have, has been built up over years of practice and experience. Where Willie has the edge over most others, however, is in that extra vision in knowing where the cue ball is going to go, what it is going to do and in reading the situation on the table from the pattern of the balls and deciding how best to play them. One of the most common complaints among amateur players is that even though they have to a degree mastered the art of potting a ball, they can never guarantee putting the cue ball where they want to.

This is normally a combination of three things. The first is not being able to control the cue ball in the shot, which we have already looked at in an earlier section. This is mainly the result of failing to understand or apply the right kind of spin. Players will swear that they put back or side spin on the ball, but don't actually know whether they are doing it or not.

The second possible problem comes from not remembering from past situations where the cue ball will go after certain types of shot. It is very important to build up a memory bank of how the cue ball responds under different conditions, otherwise you will never be able to plan for your next shot or make the necessary adjustments if you do play a specific shot incorrectly.

The third problem comes from not being able to read the table. And here there is no real way in which you can be taught, since this ability comes from practice, trial and error and as much experience of competitive play as you can get. To a degree you can get quite a lot of guidance from watching better players and seeing how they respond to different situations – how they gain position, how they cope with awkward reds, when they split the pack, etc.

Obviously there is no single right or wrong way of playing for position. In this section Willie discusses the principles involved in positional snooker and the things you should consider when making your choice of shot. He looks at the different ways in which you can 'read' the table from the situation of the balls and also other factors that can affect the run of the ball, such as the nap of the cloth.

When it comes to planning what shot to play, the one word you should keep firmly in your mind is adaptability. I believe it is a great mistake ever to approach a match with a game plan in your head and try to play to that. You can only play to the situation on the table and that on the scoreboard, bearing in mind of course the way the game has been going. The better and more quickly you can adapt, the more successful you will be.

PLANNING SHOTS

BY WILLIE THORNE

Winning at snooker is, of course, all about scoring points and every player tries to do this with as few visits to the table as possible. I will be discussing the question of break-building later, but to do this successfully you must plan your shots in advance. Although there have been players who literally take one ball at a time, because they have difficulty with positional play, you will never be able to build up reasonable breaks consistently this way.

However carefully you do plan the next few shots, there is always the chance that something will go wrong. You may mis-hit slightly or get a bad kiss on the ball and consequently fail to gain the position you were after. Then you will need to reassess the situation and possibly alter your plan. But it is important to think ahead – at least two or three balls, anyway – if you ever hope to build up a decent break.

In order to gain position for your next shot, you will have to have mastered the various aspects of ball control and have a reasonable selection of shots available. You must also be able to work out angles, not only those for potting but also when running off a cushion. You will also have to assess the condition of the table itself and any idiosyncracies it may have and take into account the different effects of the nap.

Not even the best players can guarantee position on every shot they play. But what they have to do is allow for a slight margin of error and plan within that allowance, maybe with an option to take on another ball if the shot doesn't work out quite as planned. The better you are at judging this aspect of the game, the longer you will stay on the table and the larger your breaks will be.

POSITIONAL PLAY

When you first start playing, you will obviously be concentrating on making the pot. Only by doing this will you put points on the board. But it is just as important to make sure you finish in the best position to play the next shot. Having potted a red, you want to be on a colour to take advantage of the situation. It doesn't end there, however, because you need the right position on that colour to get on another red afterwards – and so on.

That is why selection of the colours is very important too. There is no point in going for a black if it makes positioning for another red impossible – unless there is nothing else on and you want to get maximum points from the break available. You will have seen the problems involved in potting a red, but then running the cue ball back down the table and losing position on the black or pink. Unless you finish up low on the blue and can naturally run through towards the reds again, you will have to play a baulk colour and bring the cue ball back up the table. Already you have made life more difficult for yourself.

PLAYING THE ANGLES

The importance of good position is highlighted by the fact that where the cue ball finishes determines the angle you have on your next pot – and you will have already discovered that some are easier than others. Equally, some offer better opportunities for position on the next shot.

You should always avoid leaving yourself with too thick or too thin a contact, since this will restrict the angle at which the cue ball can come off the object ball. Where you have a full-ball pot, you are limited to a position somewhere on the line of the shot, depending on whether you run through, stun or screw back. Equally you have little choice with a thin cut as to where you can finish with the cue ball.

The ideal angles are either a half or threequarter-ball, since even playing a plain-ball shot you give yourself a wide range of positions from it. And this is always the shot to choose in preference, since you can allow the cue ball to run naturally after contact and minimise the risk of error. More problems are likely when you deliberately have to alter the direction of the cue ball by playing with spin.

I personally prefer to be on a half-ball, particularly when playing the black. As the cue ball naturally runs off the top cushion, all I have to worry about is where exactly I want to hit the pack of reds to split them.

Understanding the angles is, I'm afraid, not something you can really be taught. It comes with years of practising and playing. Although I rarely play billiards now, this is quite a good way of judging angles, both round the table and off the object ball when playing a cannon.

My advice to anyone learning the game is to get used to those angles you understand and are happiest playing. Once you have reached the stage of making

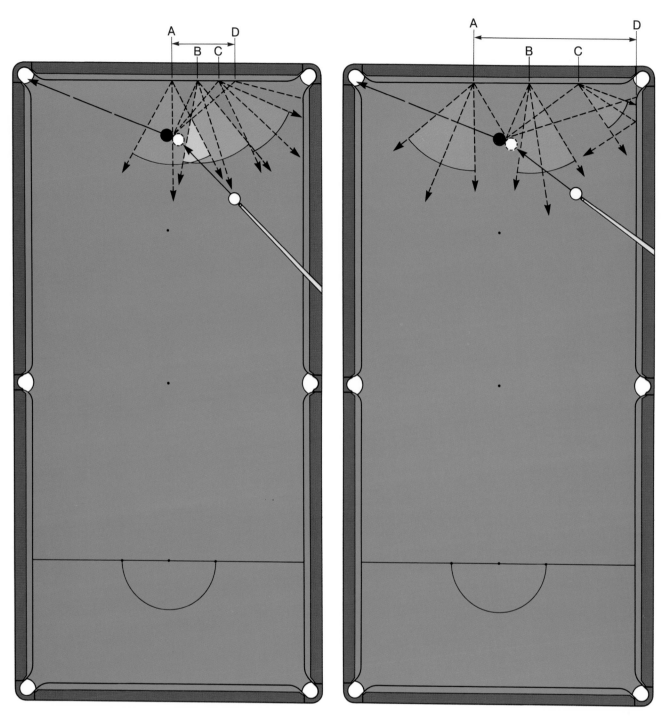

The purpose of these two illustrations is to show how the angle you have on a shot can affect the range of position you can gain off it. I have taken the black as an example, because this is the colour you would normally try to play off to create a high-scoring break. With the first example, I have shown a half-ball pot and you can see quite clearly from the area of cushion the cue ball will make contact with what scope you have in terms of finding position for the next shot. Points A-D indicate where on the top cushion you can send the cue ball, with the middle arrow showing the path of the cue ball with a plain-ball strike, the left-hand arrow that with maximum left-hand side and the right-hand arrow that with maximum right-hand side. Point A is for a centre-ball shot, B for a stun shot, C for a screw shot and D for a shot with maximum screw. Using exactly the same procedure for the second illustration, you can see how much greater the choice of position when you are playing a threequarter-ball pot.

regular 20 or 30–breaks and are confident about your potting, you can then begin to learn the possible extent of different angles and the effect these have.

READING THE TABLE

The conditions under which you play should also affect how you plan your shots, since they can make a big difference in a variety of ways. The atmosphere may be damp or there may be a particular roll on the table, either of which can alter the desired effect of a shot.

A good example is where you are on a table that rolls, possibly an inch or so to the right. Immediately your shot becomes that much harder because one of the ways to counteract it is to apply side. This is where powerful back spin players come into their own. One of the best ways of controlling the run of the cue ball when the table rolls to one side or the cloth is damp is to use back spin.

Normally I would have no problems in playing a stun shot and running through with the cue ball, but in damp conditions I find this virtually impossible to do with any degree of accuracy. Players like Jimmy or Neal can put sufficient power into the shot to screw back, not only giving them good contact but also positional control as well.

This is where, as an amateur or at club level, players are at a distinct disadvantage. At the professional level, we rarely encounter such adverse conditions and can usually play our normal game. In a local hall or snooker club the tables are unlikely to be in perfect condition, either because there is a roll or the cloth is worn or the place itself is damp. The more you try to do things with the cue ball, the tougher it becomes.

To overcome these problems, you will have to restrict yourself to plain-ball shots as much as possible, which necessarily is good practice but does limit your game. If, for example, you attempted to play with side, you would have to use more power in the shot and the more chance there would be of pushing the cue ball too far off line.

The same principle applies when you are playing on a table with tight pockets. This makes dead centre potting absolutely essential and the easiest way to achieve this is by using plain-ball shots whenever possible.

It is in such situations that players like Steve, Terry or Dennis would be at a distinct advantage. They would naturally concentrate on keeping their game simple and build up smaller breaks. Someone like myself would always be looking to score more and therefore be tempted to take a more ambitious approach. As a result we would find ourselves struggling to keep control of the cue ball and good position on the table.

JUDGING THE NAP

The nap of the cloth runs from the baulk end to the top of the table and, depending on which way you are playing the cue ball and the effect you put on it, the nap can react in different ways. You need to be able to judge this effect to ensure accurate striking.

When playing up the table, the nap will tend to take the cue ball in the same direction as any side put on it. This means that with left-hand side the cue ball will travel to the left and vice-versa. But playing against the nap has a totally different effect, since the cue ball will tend to travel away from the centre of the table. So even if you play the cue ball with left-hand side, it will tend to move to the right – and vice-versa.

You have to be particularly careful about the effect of the nap when playing safety shots as to where the cue ball will finish up, remembering that the slower you play them, the greater the 'roll' effect will be. This can be to your advantage where you are playing from the top cushion and can only use a thin contact. Using side, you can run the ball up comfortably behind one of the baulk colours. Otherwise your only option would have been to play off the cushion.

This is a shot that a lot of amateurs would probably not even consider. The normal shot would be to play a thicker contact and use one or two cushions to end up behind the baulk colours. But you can gain the same effect without using the cushions, simply by playing ths shot more slowly and using side.

This use of side against the nap is not that common because normally players would look to put the cue ball as close to the bottom cushion as possible rather than go for a snooker. Also, the pace of the shot is critical to gain the best position.

An interesting tactical point arises here, since often it is more difficult to play off the cushion safely than

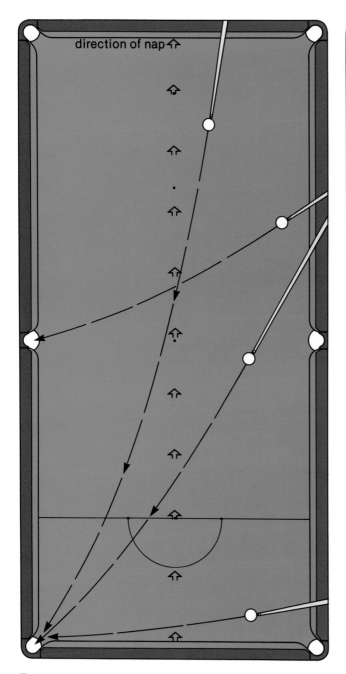

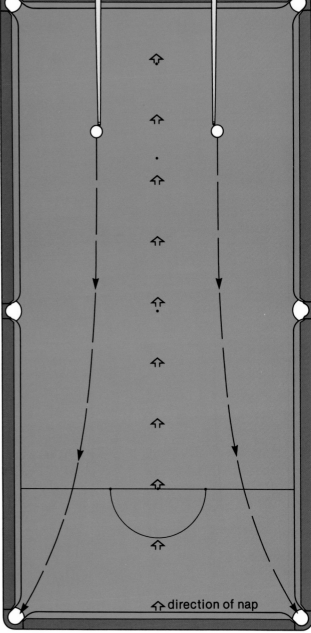

The nap of the cloth runs from the baulk to the top of a table. Depending on whether you are playing with or against the nap, over a long distance the cue ball will be affected in different ways.

In the first illustration you can see that if you are playing against the nap, the cue ball is travelling against the cloth and will tend to run away from the centre of the table. In the second illustration,

again against the nap, you will notice how the cue ball tends to run in the opposite direction to the side put on it – that is, with left-hand side it will run to the right and vice-versa. When play-

ing with side with the nap, the effect tends to be exaggerated and the nap will in effect help the direction of the spin.

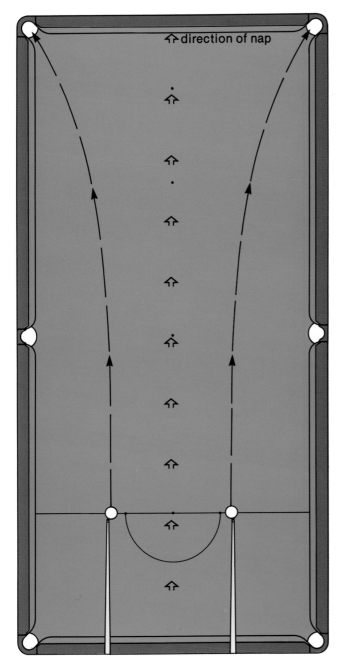

direction of nap

opponent on the baulk cushion he then has to hit a red and find an escape route to the baulk.

The nap can play a significant part in a game, particularly if you are not a power player, and you should therefore study its effects and understand how to counteract these when necessary.

PLAYING WITH SIDE

As I mentioned earlier, with snooker at any level you should always try to play to your strengths. If you can do this, it will make shot selection a lot easier, since you will normally be playing to get position for the type of shot you prefer. As has already been mentioned in the book, I rarely play a plain-ball shot. There is nearly always a trace of side on every shot I play.

I think one of the main reasons for this is that, when I first started playing, the tables I used were in pretty poor shape. I soon realised that to know exactly what the ball was going to do I had to put side on it. Having spent so long playing this way, I now find it extremely difficult to play a plain-ball shot.

There are several disadvantages of playing this way. Probably the most critical is that to use side effectively you must be striking the ball very sweetly. If you are not cueing well, it is very difficult to judge exactly how much side you are using and you are therefore quite likely to miss the shot. Even if your cueing action is not as perfect as you would like, at least with plain-ball striking you have a much better chance of success.

A good example of this is with the long pot, where the object ball is hanging over the pocket. I would always play this shot fractionally thick, because I know I am going to put a bit of side on it. Normally this would transfer itself slightly and make the object ball kick over a bit, ensuring the pot even if I was slightly off target. But if I put too much side – or none at all – on the cue ball, I would certainly miss the pot.

It is at times like this that I wish I could play plain balls, because at least then you know exactly where you have to hit the cue ball and you simply aim at where you need to strike the object ball to pot it. Because I use side and therefore have to aim thicker or thinner, if I strike the cue ball wrong I inevitably jaw the object ball.

Another problem when using side can be with the

to play a snooker. Where the reds are comparatively undisturbed, it is a relatively simple shot to leave the cue ball in amongst them, having played off a side cushion. The added advantage here is that there is the chance of a touching ball, which means you will then have to look for a safety shot. If you leave your

cue tip. When it is new it acts so differently and I find I need to play it in for several hours before I can use side effectively. So one of the secrets of playing with side is knowing your tip.

I find the weight of the cue makes quite a difference as well. It needs to be on the heavier side – around 17½ oz. If I played with a lighter cue I wouldn't get nearly as much side as I do. My cue is also fairly rigid, which I think helps too. You certainly don't want one that has any whip on it.

One of the most useful shots with side is when potting a long red from around the baulk end, as I have just mentioned. The normal way to play this is with plenty of power and back spin so that the cue ball screws back up the table towards the baulk colours.

Because I would tend to play for the black – or possibly the pink – I need to control the cue ball and get it on to one of these colours. If you simply played it with some top spin, the cue ball would just bounce off the red and end up somewhere on the cushion. By using dragging side, which means a low contact, the cue ball will drift on towards the black. It's a very useful shot to play, but carries with it a high degree of risk since you must pot the red!

So, as you can see, side can be a great friend – or a disastrous enemy. If you can master it, use it. But plain-ball striking should always be the first choice.

SHOT SELECTION

One of the hardest aspects of playing tournament snooker is deciding when to go for a shot and when to play safe. Dennis will be looking at this in more detail later in the book, but there are a few points I would like to make in the context of planning your shots.

The important point to consider when you are in this situation is weighing up your chances of making the shot against the potential dangers of the situation at the time. If, for example, I am 33 points ahead with one red left and I am faced with a difficult pot but one that I would normally achieve more times

than not, then I would definitely have to go. What would help me in this decision is the fact that my opponent would still need to take a pink or black with the red if I did miss it, which of course makes it more difficult for him, added to which he would then need to gain good position for the yellow.

Naturally if you were on a big break, you would not hesitate to go for the shot. Equally, if you were 30 odd points behind and had a chance of finishing on the black you would normally try the shot, simply because it might be your last opportunity in that frame.

These are all positive situations. You may, alternatively, be in a situation where there is a 50/50 pot but position on the black was not guaranteed. In this case you might decide to play for a snooker to try and force an error from your opponent.

In most cases, it's a question of weighing up the chances against the possible consequences and deciding on that basis whether to take a positive or more cautious approach.

The rhythm of your play at the time can also be a determining factor. If you have been playing a series of relatively straightforward shots, your confidence is high and you find it is much easier to drop into a rhythm. As a result you stand a much better chance of playing a trickier shot successfully.

Equally you may have to work hard for every point, continually doing things with the cue ball to cope with awkward shots. In this situation it is very difficult to get any sort of rhythm going. Then suddenly you play one good shot and you find you have rediscovered it – and you are away again.

Of course the initial pot is always important to set you up for a break. After that, the next 15 or 20 points have little significance, because you will usually need at least half-a-dozen shots before you drop into your rhythm. How often do you see a player break down after 20 or 30 points? It is only at this stage normally that he will start to settle down and would then be looking for a frame-winning score.

So the lesson to be learnt here is not to be too ambitious with your shot selection until you have played yourself in.

Usually there is an infinite number of ways to play a break in a given situation and every player will have his own style and approach to this. What you must always try to do is play to your strengths, something that you tend to do naturally in your choice of individual shots, rather than deliberately plan for over the duration of the break.

Normally there is more than one way of playing a particular shot, both or any of which you can argue to be right for the situation. Depending on which one you go for, the pattern and style of the break will vary from then on. It is interesting to see that certain players will always tend to play a break a particular type of way and this is something they do subconsciously. This is fine until they find themselves out of position and more often than not the break comes to an end. The best break-builders are those who can adapt and, if necessary, change direction midway, depending on the state of the balls. That, of course, is dependant on the range of shots they have at their disposal.

Where Willie can be so devastating in his break-building is in his close positional play in the top half of the table, especially around the pink and black. This is a most important area to practise on, as Willie emphasises, and to be able to play yourself back into should you temporarily lose position.

Accurate position off the pot is, of course, all important too. The less times you leave yourself cueing off the cushion or over another ball, the greater the chance of making big breaks, which are your best guarantee of winning frames - and therefore matches.

BREAK BUILDING

BY WILLIE THORNE

Once you have mastered the basic techniques involved with cue and ball control and are confident about potting, not only in a straight line but also at an angle, and you have grasped the principles of being able to control the cue ball after a pot to position yourself for the next shot, then you can start concentrating on building up a break. This, after all, is how you win matches.

I firmly believe that temperament and mental approach are the two most important elements in snooker and account for the reasons why a good player either succeeds or fails in a match situation. Obviously one has to accept that the player has reached a standard of play where the range of shots necessary can be played consistently and well. But that alone will not win matches.

Break building is probably my greatest asset and I have developed this skill by constant practice, not so much on my shot technique but by concentrating on clearing the table. Doubtless this accounts for the fact that I have scored more maximums than any other professional in the game today – 80 at the last count.

I am sure this has been helped by my positive attitude when I get to the table, whether through having played a good safety shot to let myself back in or because my opponent has missed or played a poor shot. Then the first thing that goes through my mind is whether there is a chance for me to get 30 or 40 points on the board, possibly a chance to win the frame or maybe make the highest break of the match.

Naturally I have to consider carefully the state of the frame at the time. Possibly it is halfway through the frame and there are five or six reds still up. I can see that there is at least a 30 or 40-point break there, but I am trailing by a similar amount. Then, of course, that break becomes very important and I know I must make sure I get it, even though I cannot see a way of winning the frame from that visit.

Alternatively it is early on in the game, with all 15 reds still on the table, but I have been left an opening. Then I will certainly think about a large break to win the frame – or at least put me in the running for the highest break award. This is what I mean by taking a positive approach, depending on the situation.

Different players will, of course, approach break-building in different ways and I suppose the key to it is whether you are in an attacking or a defensive

mood. As I have said, my attitude has been set by my approach to practising. When I am not playing particularly well, I will go through the whole range of shots, rather than just concentrate on the one or two that may be letting me down. That is why I tend to use the 'line-up' exercise quite a lot, since I believe this helps get your cueing going well.

I have to admit that I am not the best player in the world for practising – particularly in the number of hours I spend at it. Most of the time I play round the black, which is why I am used to scoring so many maximums. The one advantage of this is that you will necessarily be giving yourself quite a lot of difficult shots to play to get back on the black after each red. But equally this provides you with a constant test of the full range of shots.

That is why I say that I would build a break in a different way to other players, since all the time I am trying to stay on the black. Even in tournaments, I would never take the cue ball down for the pink or blue or any of the baulk colours unless I really had to. I concentrate on playing round the black until I lose position.

The important thing for anyone, at whatever level of the game, is to make sure you win the frame. This is particularly critical early on, when there are plenty of reds on the table. Even if you only make a 30 or 40-point break and then play safe, this is much better than being tempted into a silly shot and giving the frame away.

When you are planning to build a break, you will obviously be playing around the pack, which in the early stages of a frame will normally be fairly well intact. Although initially you will work your way round the loose reds, if any, there comes a stage where you have to play the cue ball into the pack to open up other reds.

This is where players who have a good power shot and control over it will be at an advantage. If I want to play into the pack, I aim to finish on a half-ball black and play either high or low to try and disturb the reds. In contrast Jimmy would try for a three-quarter-ball angle on the black to enable him to screw into the pack, using check side. Jimmy can impart so much power into this shot that, with the spin, it goes again and forces its way into the pack, spreading the reds much more.

That is why, because I don't have the same cue

power, I have to position myself lower or higher on the black in order to get the cue ball to do all the work through the angle rather than through power in the spin. It is the same with a long deep screw shot up the table. I would normally have to go for a stun shot to play on to a baulk colour or screw the cue ball to get on to the pink.

I mention such examples to give you an idea of how your ability to play certain shots can affect the way in which you build up a break, since this is all about position on the cue ball. You will learn from practice and experience what your limitations are and how you should go about setting up a successful break.

I know some of my colleagues would not agree with my methods of coaching, but for anyone who had mastered the basic techniques I would get them to play the 'line-up' as much as possible. I used to play it for hours and hours to build up my score. After making 40s, 50s and 60s, I then built this up to 70s, 80s and 90s. Although this is not quite the same as a match situation, since you are not getting awkward balls to play, for example on the cushion, it does help your cueing technique and angled potting no end.

As a professional, playing the line-up I would reckon to clear the table nine times out of 10. A good amateur should be looking for a score in the 60s or 70s. This is equivalent to a break of about 30 or 40 in normal conditions. And the exercise includes virtually all the shots you would normally have to play when building up a break – little stun, screw and run-through shots.

Tactics vary, too, between players when building up a break. If I have one or two balls on the cushion, I tend to move them earlier than most other professionals. When exactly you play for that little kiss that will bring them back into play is down to you. But you should always make sure that you land up on another ball. This, of course, doesn't matter when the frame is won. But early on in the break, when there are still plenty of reds, it could well be disastrous if you are forced to end the break and let your opponent in.

Before I move balls off the cushion, I always try to make sure I have left an alternative ball near a pocket. This guarantees that even if I do get an awkward kiss – and maybe leave the cue ball on the cushion – I still have the option of a relatively simple next shot. That's why I will move these balls while I still have other reds on.

The alternative, of course, is to leave the tricky shots till last and make sure you build up a sizeable break. In some cases you may find you don't need that other ball and, even if you do and you are forced to end the break, you have left an awkward shot for your opponent.

Certainly my advice to anyone starting to build up breaks is to try and give yourself a choice of reds whenever you can. By playing for more than one red, you may end up in a slightly worse position, but you are increasing the chances of continuing that break and, equally important, keeping your options open. In time you will have the confidence to play for just one red in the knowledge that you should get good position from it for the next colour.

I tend to play for more than one red as often as possible to ensure I have a choice of angles to get back on the black. Obviously this might not apply in a tournament situation, since I would not necessarily be trying for a maximum and would take, for example, a pink or blue if that gave me a better position for the next red.

Normally I would look to put the frame out of reach every time I saw the chance of a reasonable break. It's all down to your attitude and how you feel at the time. If you are playing well, it all can seem very easy. When you aren't, it becomes so difficult.

So what should be going through your mind when you get to the table? Obviously you don't stand there and try to work out the possible value of the break or necessarily whether you can clear the table at that stage. It depends very much on the state of the frame – and the match, for that matter.

You should, of course, be looking for the maximum amount of points. But it's only towards the end of the frame, when there are possibly two or three reds left, that you have to start thinking about how you should play it. If you feel you can win the frame from this position, then you should be looking to clear the table. If the situation is very tight, you could set up a snooker to put your opponent in trouble.

It's more a question of weighing up the overall situation, rather than counting points. For the average player would only be looking two or three shots ahead – for the pot, then a colour and position on the next red.

How exactly you play a break depends on the individual and naturally on how the balls are positioned. As I said, when there are balls on the cushion, I would be looking to move them very early on. So I would plan my shots to get a good angle to do this. Where these are at the top end of the table, you should try to get on the pink or black and work from there. There is no point in trying to move them when you are down among the baulk colours, because you are giving yourself too difficult a shot.

There are times when you have an awkward path through to the balls you want. Again, I would try to play to clear the balls in the way and thus open up the table for the rest. So all the time you are manoeuvring for good position and, I believe, you should give yourself the maximum opportunity to do this, rather than leave it for the last few reds. On the one hand you are in danger of opening up the game for your opponent if you miss a shot. But equally you will be reducing your chances if you leave it to the last moment.

It is interesting to look at how the approach of the Matchroom players varies in this situation. Steve, for example, is a very methodical player and would tend to leave a ball on the cushion until he has got the frame won. Dennis and Terry normally play the same way. Jimmy, Neal and Tony would try to play the awkward ball earlier.

I do find that the more methodical players tend to frighten me less than those who play with more flair and are therefore more unpredictable. With Terry and Dennis – and possibly Tony as well – you accept that if they get in among the balls they are quite likely to make a century break. All you can do is wait and hope that they miss a shot or lose position. In contrast, Jimmy and Neal can suddenly come up with a brilliant clearance and as you watch them play you are wondering whether you will get another shot.

I believe it is most important for successful break-building to plan to play to your strengths. This is why, if the black is tied up, I would tend to play safety shots until I could release it, because I know that from the way I have practised over the years that this is where I am going to score most heavily.

Because I have basically developed my cue ball control using the three cushions at the top of the table, I will be in more trouble if the black comes down the table around the middle of the side

cushions than if it is near its spot – even though it may temporarily be out of commission.

This highlights an important aspect of the game, which as a developing player you should concentrate on. Although you will discover your strengths and should obviously play to them, you also need to build up all-round skills so that you can play on any part of the table. You may find that you cannot score so much on individual breaks, but several smaller ones can win you the frame just as much as a century can.

Temperament and concentration are a vital part of break-building, which is why Steve wins so consistently. He can happily play a series of small breaks and build up a score gradually, whereas players like Jimmy and I always want to see the balls going in. If we miss several on the trot, we start to think we are playing badly and this puts us off. With Steve – and Terry and Dennis, as well – being off form doesn't automatically mean losing frames. When things aren't going right, they will concentrate on a simple, solid approach, just taking the points where they can and waiting their opportunity.

One of the problems of being a regular high-break player – and, believe me, they do exist! – is that once I get under way I do not expect to lose position very often. When I do, therefore, I tend to get very annoyed with myself.

In a way, those players who do not concentrate so much on position don't suffer the same problem. If they do gain good position, so much the better. But if the cue ball ends up on one of the cushions, they simply play the next available shot, even if this means rolling the ball along the cushion to get the pot.

The fact that I had played such a poor positional shot would tend to upset me and, of course, that in turn puts me under more pressure for the next one. Because you played for that position and it doesn't work out perfectly, you can easily lose a little confidence – and that, of course, can be fatal.

When you are on a century or more break, you are generally going to be out of position at least a couple of times. An element of luck – and misfortune, for that matter – often comes into it and you must have the resilience to get down and play on as though nothing had happened. This is where the positive approach is so important. You have to believe with every shot that you will get it and forget the fact that it is particularly difficult or awkward.

I remember in the 1985 UK Championships I played really well throughout the tournament and had convinced myself that I was the best player there. My mental attitude could not have been better and every time I got to the table I knew I was going to get a 60 or 70-break. I went into the last session of the final 13–8 ahead – and I was playing Steve, too!

I kept saying to myself that I only needed to win the next frame after the interval and I was there. Even when I was 40 behind, I went into the break thinking I could clear up to take the frame. I got as far as the brown – and then missed the blue. I eventually lost 16–14, but it was a tremendous final with both Steve and I playing extremely well.

Although Steve did beat me in the end, I am sure that it was my positive attitude that took me to within a whisker of the title. This illustrates well why Steve has been so successful over the years. His attitude and temperament are such that he will recover from seemingly impossible situations. Even when he is not playing well, he has the capacity to win. That is the quality of champions.

I went through a bad spell in 1979 and 1980 and, looking back, I can only blame it on a lack of positive approach. I got myself into the state where I thought that if I missed a shot I had lost. This couldn't have been better highlighted by the fact that in three matches – against Eddie Charlton, Bill Werbenuik and John Virgo – I was three frames up and needing one more for victory and unbelievably lost them all.

The lesson is there for everyone to learn, at whatever level of the game. Prepare yourself mentally for each match, don't be annoyed when you miss a shot and always think positively. The better you feel, the better you will play.

It's hard to explain, but it is an interesting aspect of playing a big break how often you fail in the following frame. Possibly because of the concentration you have put into that particular frame, you then tend to relax on the next one and let your opponent in. I remember well in a match against Alex Higgins some years ago I made four century breaks, including a 143 – and still lost, so it is important to bear in mind that big breaks may win you frames, but they don't guarantee you the match.

Break-building is definitely something you develop after years of practice and experience. When you start off, you must concentrate on your technique, without which you will never score consistently. Gradually you will find you are putting together 20s and 30s, then maybe 40s and 50s. But eventually you will realise that without the full range of shots – for example screw shots with reverse, running or check side, stuns and run-throughs – you will not be able to keep a reasonable break going.

That is why I recommend the line-up as a good form of practice to master these shots. You can start to set yourself targets – going for 15 blues, then 15 pinks and finally 15 blacks. This, of course, is extremely difficult to do. But it is practices like this that help you develop a sound technique for break-building and one that I have found very valuable.

CENTURY BREAK

I put together the following break, which was a table clearance of 133, to illustrate what approach you need to take when at the table and how you can work out ways of building up a large break shot by shot, depending on the position of the balls and how you end up after each shot. As I have played from one situation to another, I have described both the options available and the reasons why I decided to take a particular route. Naturally there were many ways of playing the break and you should therefore only use this as an example of how to build and consider the choices of shot available. The accumulative score is shown in the bottom right-hand corner of each picture.

0

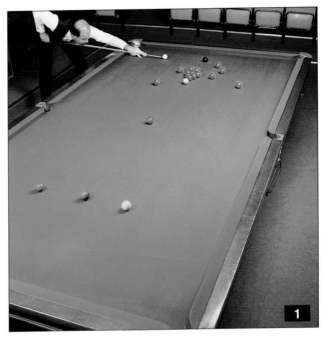

1

Having played a poor break-off shot, my opponent left me in with a long red, from which I could then get on the black. This is by no means an easy shot, since I must make the pot, while stopping the cue ball virtually dead for position on the black.

I have finished up with a good angle on the black from which I can stun the cue ball into the reds. Hopefully I will move some of the reds out but will still be on one of the two loose reds for my next pot into the top right-hand pocket.

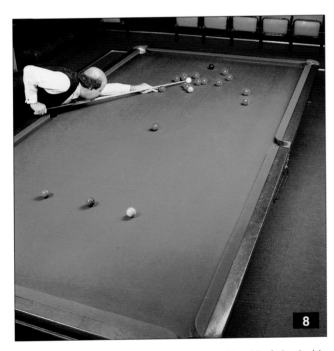

8

9

Having potted the red, I've left myself a nice half-ball angle on the black, which will give me a choice of several reds. I will aim to play the cue ball off the top cushion with a bit of check side to bring it back into the reds. Even if I don't get the right kiss on them, I will still have a choice of two reds into either top pocket.

With the last shot I managed to bring four or five into play by stunning off the black and still finished up on the red I wanted to pot into the top right-hand pocket. For this shot, all I need to do is roll the red in and come off the top cushion for the black. Here I need a slight angle to make sure I can then get on to a choice of three or four reds afterwards.

The cue ball kissed the reds as I wanted, which has left me a straightforward red into the top right-hand pocket. All I need do here is roll the ball in again, making sure I finish on an angle for the black to leave me further choice with the next reds.

Unfortunately I finished a bit too straight on the black, although there is still a slight angle. I will try to stun off the black into the nearest red to leave me a simple pot into the top pocket. If I miss the kiss I'll still have two other reds into the other corner pocket. This means I've a possible choice of three reds with the same shot.

I played a poor shot there and the cue ball kissed the red too fully. Fortunately I do have another red into the middle left-hand pocket. This is a bit more difficult because if I just roll it in I'll be on a bad angle for the black. I will therefore try to screw back about 18 in to leave myself with a half-ball black. You should always avoid finishing straight on the black, since otherwise position becomes that much more difficult. Although there is no real problem here, I have just made the next shot that much harder than it might have been.

I've potted the red but screwed back a little too far, finishing rather straighter on the black than I wanted. However there is now a loose red between the pink and blue which will go into the middle right-hand pocket. To play for this, I can just screw back off the cushion. In this position, there is no chance of playing for more than one red, since this one is the only red that will really pot.

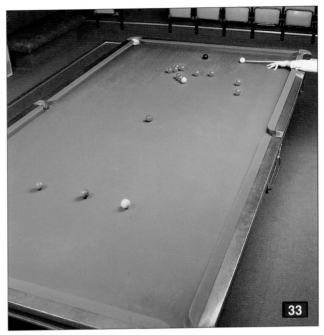

I have managed to get the angle on the red I played for, which leaves me a choice of pink or black for the next colour. By playing the stun shot I can get back through the two reds on to the black and, even if I kiss one, I'm not too worried because I will still be on the pink into the middle pocket.

Having played for the black, I've finished up at a good angle which will give me a choice of two or three reds next shot. By stunning off the black I will hope to run the cue ball through the two reds above. Even if I kiss them I will still have a good choice.

I didn't kiss the reds as fully as I would have liked and the cue ball has run back further than I wanted. Fortunately I still have the two reds on the right and can reach them with the help of the rest. By potting into the top right-hand corner I can get back on to the black.

I've ended up with a nice half-ball black into the top left-hand pocket. By playing this with a little check side, I can straighten the cue ball as it comes off the top cushion and hopefully bring it back through the two reds to finish around the pink spot. This will give me one of the three reds I went for before.

48

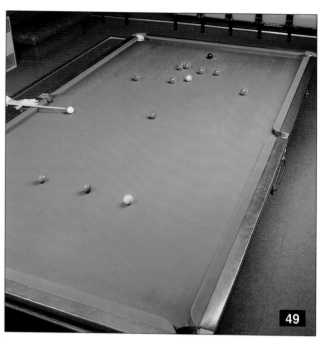

49

Where the cue ball has finished up has left me with more possibilities for the next shot. There's a red into the middle pocket, which is a simple pot but I haven't got quite the right angle to get back on to the black. Again with the two right-hand reds I cannot get the ideal position on the black. I could, of course, play a stun shot to get on the blue. But there is another shot on, which would enable me to thin out the group of four reds. It is a good idea to free reds when you get the chance and by potting the outside one I will be able to play the other three later. By stunning up through the two nearest reds I can get on the blue, but I need to make sure I finish baulk side. Otherwise I will have to run the cue ball in and out of baulk to get back on a red.

The shot I played worked out very well and I've got a nice threequarter-ball blue. From this angle I have a choice of three or four reds. This time I'll just roll the blue in and play for the red next to the pink. This will then clear the pink in case I need to use it later.

54

55

The cue ball hasn't finished up quite where I wanted it, but I will still go for the red near the pink. This time I can play for the blue or black. The first is more difficult since I must screw back far enough to finish baulk side of the blue. The easier shot is to run through for the black off the side cushion, hopefully finishing on an angle to get on the next red.

I've finished a little too straight on the black here, which has created a more difficult situation. To gain position on a red, I will have to play a forcing shot with side, taking the cue ball round two cushions and back towards the pink. This should leave me on the outside of the two middle reds. With the pace I'll be using, if I miss the kiss on the pink the cue ball should run on for the left-hand red into the top pocket. So again I've given myself a choice of more than one red.

I got the pot all right, but didn't quite achieve either of the other objectives. I didn't get a kiss on the pink and the cue ball didn't run far enough for the left-hand red. This means using the rest and going for the blue, since the angle is all wrong for the black. I'll be playing a stun shot with left-hand side off the cushion back into the middle of the table, hopefully just below the blue. The rest makes this shot a bit harder.

Though I say it myself, I played the shot rather well and now have a perfect angle on the blue.

This time I'll play a little stun shot round the table to come in by the pink for the red nearest to it.

I've played this shot a bit too hard and overrun the red to get through to the black next shot. This means going back for the blue again. At this stage I need to start thinking about the three reds in a cluster. To move them out I want a half-ball angle on either the black or pink. So now I'm thinking three or four shots ahead, instead of two.

I've gone a bit lower on the blue than I wanted, but I've still got the angle to play into the reds. The way the reds are set, I will have to allow for a little luck in how they break. But I'm in a position where I may not have another chance to get at them. In potting the blue, I will be using a little stun with right-hand side and aiming to hit the first of the reds full on, hopefully pushing the outside red towards the top left-hand pocket. You can play this shot plain ball, but Jimmy and I always use a bit of side.

74

75

Although I hit the outside red and not the centre one, it has worked out very well. That red has run towards the top pocket and the other two are now free to be potted. From here I should be able to clear the table. The red is dead straight, so all I need do is stop the cue ball for a three-quarter-ball black.

I've finished in a good position for the black and don't have to worry about playing for a choice of reds. All I have to do is run the cue ball down towards the pink spot and even if I kiss the pink I can still take one of the reds. The only danger is playing it too hard and snookering myself in front of the pink.

82

83

I played the shot harder than I planned but fortunately I'm still on the middle red into the top right-hand pocket. By using a little stun shot with left-hand side, I can push the cue ball behind the two reds to finish on the black again.

The shot went well and has given me the right angle on the black to play for the red near the right-hand cushion. The other two reds can only pot into the top right-hand pocket, anyway. By rolling the black in and coming off the cushion just a few inches I should be on for the red into the opposite middle pocket.

90

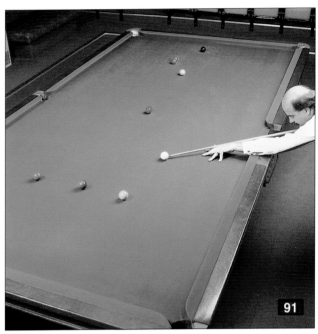

91

I would have gone for the blue next, but I've not finished with the best of angles for this. So I'll roll the red in and play for either the brown or green. What I have to make sure is that I have a good half-ball angle on one of these in order to screw back behind the reds for a pot into the top right-hand pocket. What I mustn't do is finish straight on either of them.

Although I didn't make the brown I have got a half to threequarter-angle on the green. To get position behind the reds I need now to play a fierce stun shot. If I played a normal stun I would bring the cue ball towards the middle pocket, while the screw shot would leave me by the blue. So I have to play a shot some-where between the two, using right-hand side, to come up the table straight rather than at an angle.

94

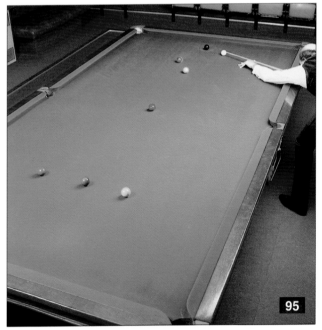

95

I succeeded in leaving the cue ball where I wanted, with a choice of either red – the left one to run through to the black or the right one to stun up for the pink. I will play for the black because if the pink is respotted it will cut down my margin for getting on to the last red. So it is a straight run-through to the black. All I need to worry about is finishing on an angle.

There is no real problem with this shot, since I have a threequarter-ball black. I can either stun off one cushion to finish high on the red or play off two cushions. With the angle I have, the easier shot is off two cushions, which I will play with a touch of top left-hand side to run the cue ball off the top and side cushion for the last red.

117

102

103

If I was playing for the highest break in a tournament, I would in this situation go for the pink next shot. Otherwise I prefer to take a baulk colour after the final red. As I haven't finished on a straight red for the pink or black, I am going to stun the cue ball through the pink and blue to get on either the brown or green. Hopefully then the colours will be a formality.

I have not finished up as high as I would have liked, since I would have preferred to play the brown. As it is, I am rather straight on the green, but there should be no problem. The only thing I must concentrate on is not screwing back more than about 18 in or I shall have to use the rest for the yellow. So I will be playing a little screw shot — anywhere from 12 in to 18 in.

106

108

I actually screwed back about 20 in – a bit more than I wanted. But fortunately I can still reach the yellow without the rest. For the green I need to screw back 12–15 in, in fact the same shot as before, but this time on the yellow.

I have left myself another easy shot. But because of the angle I need on the brown to get on the blue, I don't want to screw back too far – no more than 2–3 in to leave a threequarter-ball brown. This would give me a stun shot up to the blue.

111

115

I didn't play the last shot too well and have left myself straight on the brown. But I can overcome this by screwing back off the cushion. Because the cue ball will be striking the cushion about 18 in down, I will need a little reverse side to bring it back closer to the blue. So my shot is a little screw with right-hand side, hopefully making a nice angle for the blue. But I must make sure to finish baulk side to get on the pink.

I finished perfectly on the blue and now have a choice. I can either roll the blue in leaving the pink into the top left-hand pocket or play a forcing stun shot for a pink into the top right-hand pocket. I prefer the stun shot in this situation, because it gives me more control over the cue ball should I get a slight kick or put on a bit of side. By playing the blue quite firmly, I should make the cue ball run down the line for the pink.

120

126

Again with the pink I have a choice. I can either roll it in slowly and come off the cushion for the black (although I won't be straight on) or I can play a forcing shot which will take the cue ball off the cushion and back the other side of the black. In this situation I would not want to do anything difficult and would rather play a safe pink to leave a more awkward black. Only the circumstances can determine which way you go. This would leave me with a threequarter-ball black for the final shot.

I haven't left myself the easiest of blacks, but I knew that when I made sure of the pink. So I can aim just to roll the ball in or go for a firmer shot just to make sure, which would be my choice if the black gave me the highest break.

This example should, I hope, be useful in helping you to understand what I have talked about in this section of the book – trying to make sure you have a choice of reds, looking more than one or two shots ahead, taking advantage of opportunities to release difficult balls before you have to play them, and so on. You can set up your own situations, but I find this type of practice is well worth doing to help make you a better break-builder.

ADVANCED SNOOKER

INTRODUCTION
BY STEVE DAVIS

We have now reached Part III and the final sections on technique in the book, including advanced ball control, speciality combination shots and a detailed discussion on the various aspects of tactical play by the master himself – Dennis Taylor. But before you start considering such refinements to your game, I believe it is most important to stress yet again that if you haven't mastered all the areas of technique so far covered, what follows will have little relevance.

When I started playing the game, like any keen young player I would experiment with shots – but only in practice when it didn't matter if I got them right or not. This discipline has stood me in good stead throughout my career. Even now I don't play to the limits of my ability during a match, since I know that the chances of playing extreme shots successfully are greatly reduced. I believe you can control a game far easier by playing within your capabilities.

I am sure that most of the top players do the same. It is very rare, for example, to see Jimmy screw back to the maximum of his ability, even though he is probably the best player in the world at this type of shot. For once you start to stretch your technique to the ultimate, it necessarily develops weaknesses, which can prove fatal in a match situation.

When I was learning, I concentrated almost entirely on hitting in a straight line and potting the ball. I only started to develop other shots – using side, running through, screwing back and playing with power – when I had not only mastered hitting the ball in a straight line, but mastered it again and again. I made sure that I could hit the ball straight so many times that I would never lose sight of this technique again.

Where people fall into the trap is by believing that the day they manage to hit the ball straight they can then try to play a power screw-back shot. I remember I was at least two years into playing the game seriously, when I knew I was never going to lose the ability of hitting straight, before I even attempted such a shot.

121

In this section Neal looks at some of the really advanced shots in the game which involve special use of side on the cue ball and playing with controlled power. But, as he will be the first to remind you, it is pointless trying to master the techniques involved here if you haven't grasped all of the other techniques, right back to the basics that Terry has explained in the very first section. All aspects of playing the game are related and dependant on an underlying ability at the most elementary stage.

Another very important point to make is that with any of the more complex or advanced shots, you must make sure in your own mind that they are necessary. This applies to any shot that requires more than plain-ball striking or, at most, medium stun or power, where you are still concentrating on virtually centre ball contact. Shots that require extra spin or extra power should only be played as a last resort, when there is no other alternative.

Having said that, it is of course useful to have as wide a range of shots in your repertoire and to practise these as much as you can when your technique allows you to. In exceptional situations you may need to call on them to get yourself out of trouble or possibly to set you up for a match-winning break.

As well as discussing the more advanced applications of side and their effects, Neal explains how to develop your power game and, as he stresses, one of the most important things to remember here is keeping your head as still as possible throughout the shot. The more power you put into a shot, the greater the chance of creating some movement in the body. But you must restrict this to the absolute minimum.

Often excessive movement is brought about through a lack of understanding as to exactly how a power shot should be played. It is not a question of speeding up the cueing action or winding yourself up for the 'big hit'. It is basically about hitting the cue ball harder, which requires much more co-ordination than a lot of people have got. This is why successful power play is limited to relatively few professionals within snooker.

ADVANCED BALL CONTROL

BY NEAL FOULDS

The range of shots included in this section can add an extra dimension to your game and enable you to take a positive approach to situations in which there would otherwise be little or no chance of progressing your break. But there is no point in attempting them until you have reached a high standard in the more basic techniques already discussed.

They all require fine judgement, perfect cueing and a level of control that will only come with many months of practice and experience. And you should certainly not attempt them in a match situation unless you are confident of playing them well.

This is often a hard discipline to follow, particularly when you play an opponent with virtually every shot in the book. You must try to ignore the fact that there is anyone else in the game and play to your own strengths. If you start to worry about what the other player is doing, you will very quickly build up an inferiority complex and that can put you off your game completely.

The same can work in reverse, where you find you can obviously play shots that your opponent can't. But just because his game is more limited than your own, you should never get complacent. You may have a more varied repertoire but that alone does not guarantee that you will win. Jimmy knows this only too well. He has a tremendous talent and can play shots that few others would dare attempt. For sheer ability, you would back him against virtually all his opponents in a big match situation. But he can still lose against a more limited player.

POTTING WITH SIDE

There are times, when I am faced with a slightly awkward pot or for some reason I am not totally confident about the shot, that I will play with a little side. The advantages of this are that you can afford a thicker contact on the object ball and it does seem to help it into the pocket. It also offers greater scope for position on the cue ball after the pot.

Some players use side much more than others. While Steve, for example, would only play with side when really necessary, I don't think there is a shot that Willie plays without it. In the end, it's down to individual technique and what suits your style of play.

One situation where the use of side definitely does help is when you are trying to pot an object ball that

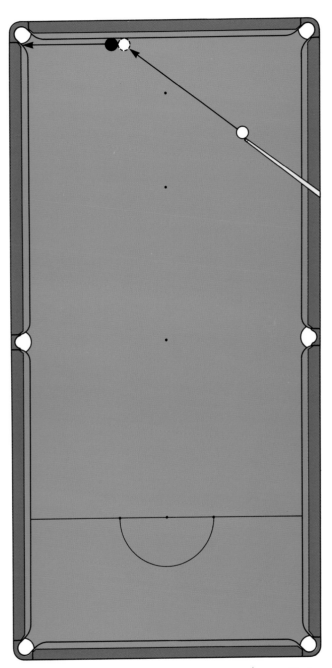

When you want to pot a ball that is on the cushion, there can be no margin for error. The safest way of playing this shot is to use side and play the cue ball to strike the cushion a fraction be- fore it makes contact with the object ball. When potting to the left, you need to use left-hand side – and vice-versa for a pot to the right.

is resting on the cushion near a pocket. The problem here is getting the right contact on the object ball to send it along the cushion, since there is absolutely no margin for error. If you strike it a fraction off line this will push it away from the cushion and you will miss the pocket by miles.

What you must aim to do is play the cue ball on to the cushion a fraction before it makes contact with the object ball. By using a little side, you will be widening the angle at which the cue ball comes off the cushion and therefore enabling it to stay on the line of the pot just that fraction longer. If you are aiming the object ball at a pocket to the right, you must use right-hand side – and vice-versa if the pocket is to the left.

This does not guarantee the pot, since your contact with the object ball has to be absolutely right, and you are also reliant on the roll along the cushion. But it will certainly increase your chances of making the pot.

The other way of playing the shot, which Jimmy for example normally uses, is to aim for half cushion and half object ball contact. But this needs precise accuracy to ensure you send the object ball in a straight line towards the pocket.

You will have to experiment with this type of pot to see which you find easier to play. While using side can help, if you are not a strong player in this respect you should always play the plain-ball shot.

TRANSMITTED SIDE

This example raises the interesting question as to whether it is possible to transmit side from the cue ball on to the object ball. There have been conflicting thoughts on this theory, but it would certainly help explain why potting along the cushion can be made easier by using side. The argument is that side is transmitted on to the object ball and helps it to hug the cushion on its way to the pocket.

Jimmy is another who believes in this theory, although he would be the first to admit that it is not something you can control. But there are occasions when it happens that you cannot put it down to just the roll of the table, as the object ball actually alters direction slightly.

There is one situation where I believe it does happen, since it has occurred to me a number of times on different tables. I have been faced with a possible pot, but have had to swerve the cue ball slightly round another ball to get on to the red I want to pot. I have played the shot with a little right-hand side on to the red, which has then run fractionally off the line I intended to play. It only seems to happen on very sensitive, lively tables when I have played a soft shot.

I know a very good amateur player who claimed that, faced with only half a pocket, he could strike the cue ball with side and get the object ball to spin in off the exposed jaw into the pocket.

Although this is a very interesting subject, it is definitely not one that you should worry about. As I said earlier, it is impossible to control and therefore not something you can confidently play for. If it does happen, then if you are lucky it will work for you. Equally it can work against you.

SCREW BACK WITH SIDE

This is one of the most difficult shots to play well, because not only are you aiming to hit the cue ball near the bottom but you also have to hit it to one side. You are therefore aiming at the least amount of ball and, in fact, are just a fraction off miscueing. You therefore need excellent technique and should only attempt the shot when you can guarantee to cue with pin-point accuracy.

The main advantage of this shot is that it opens up a far greater range of positions. But you have to remember that because you are playing with screw as well, the effect of the side will reverse the direction of the cue ball after the strike. This is one good reason why this shot should not be used until you are fully conversant with the effect of spin and the range of control on the cue ball. The natural reaction in this situation would be to hit the cue ball on the side you wanted it to run on after contact. In fact, the opposite is the case, unless you are playing a dead straight shot.

The interesting thing about this situation is that you can use side to change the angle at which the cue ball runs on after contact. I have noticed Steve playing this shot and I do occasionally as well, which can be extremely effective when you are looking for a particular position on the next shot.

Because of the difficulty of this shot, I normally

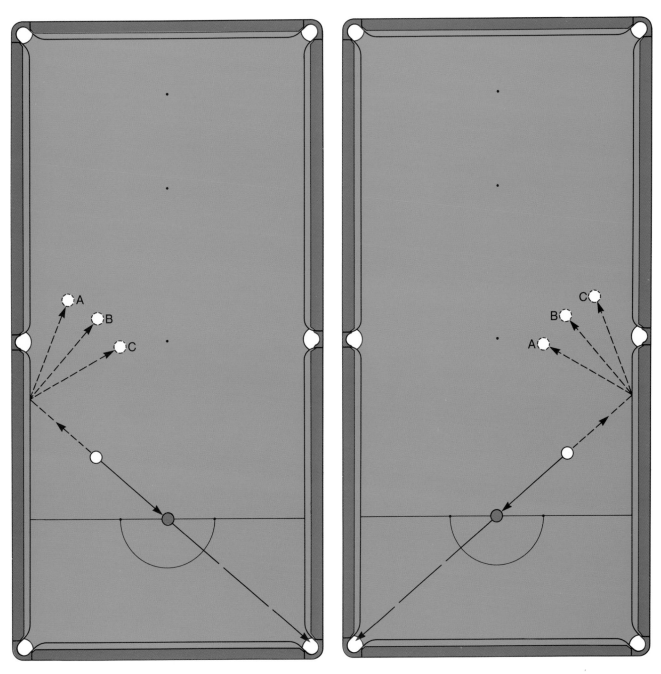

A good way to understand the effect of reverse side is to use these illustrations, where you have a full-ball pot on the brown into the bottom corner pockets. In the first example, where you are potting the brown into the right-hand bottom pocket, A indicates the direction the cue ball will travel when playing with back spin and right-hand side, B the direction with just back spin and C the direction with back spin and left-hand side. If you then play the same pot but from the other side of the table, you will see how the effect of the side spin is reversed, so that A is the direction with left-hand side and C that with right-hand side. What you need to bear in mind with back spin and side is that the cue ball will run off the cushion in the opposite direction to the side put on it.

only play it when I have a fairly short, easy pot on – say from up to 2 ft. Even then, you have got to be hitting the ball very well. I certainly wouldn't attempt it from more than 4 ft. away from the object ball. The further the cue ball has to travel, the less the effect of side on the ball, since it wears off quite quickly. And you will need extreme side to ensure that it still takes effect once it makes contact with the object ball and then the cushion.

There are some players who would never use this shot, mainly because they do not want to miss the opportunity of the pot, which is understandable.

The best time to play this shot is when you are going for the black on or near its spot and want to screw into the pack to split the reds. This situation is very common in matchplay. Jimmy is an expert at this, but he tends to use check side, putting a lot more power into the shot. If you can master this technique, it can become a very important part of the game. Should the reds break well, you can win the frame from this position.

The difference between simply screwing off the black and screwing with check side can be dramatic. Without side, the cue ball will run into the pack, but often the reds hardly move. With side, and particularly check side, there is far more chance of the reds scattering, because the cue ball is forcing its way through the pack rather than screwing into it and then out again.

Again, it is important to understand how the effect of the spin works, because you actually hit the opposite side to that which would help the object ball into the pocket. So if you are potting into the right pocket you would use left-hand side – and right-hand side to pot into the left pocket.

Particularly with check side, you must be behind the black – or parallel to it – and you must be in a good position for the pot. You really are pumping the ball into the pack and therefore must have the cue power to do this. Whereas with a simple screw shot there is always an element of luck as to where the reds go and whether or not you bury the cue ball in the pack, using check side is the most certain way of spreading the reds and leaving a shot on. If you do it well, it gives you a tremendous feeling. But it is a very hard shot and you have to be confident to play it in a match – and only then after weeks of practice.

I would say that you have to be of a very high

From this illustration you can see how check side is used on the cue ball to help split up the pack of reds. This is a shot that Jimmy, in particular, plays very well. The half-ball black has provided a good angle and by using right-hand side and bottom on the cue ball, the effect is to take it into the reds after contact with the black. Because there is side spin on the ball, this helps take it through the reds, spreading them at the same time. With just back spin, the cue ball tends to hit the reds and then come back towards the top cushion. This shot makes the pot much more difficult.

standard as an amateur to take on this kind of shot. If you attempt it too early, you will probably, as Jimmy says, end up with broken cues and torn cloths! Certainly he should know, since he – and Tony – are the best at it. There are many professsionals who wouldn't even consider trying it.

A good example of just how well Jimmy plays this type of shot came in the 1984 Benson & Hedges Masters against Kirk Stevens, when in fact the Canadian made a maximum 147 in front of the cameras. Jimmy played a pink with screw and side off three cushions. When it hit one cushion it had reverse side, when it hit the next it had running side, which stopped it, and then unbelievably it found life again and ran on! Only Jimmy could play a shot like that.

POWER SHOTS

I touched on cue power when I was talking about screwing with check side to run into the pack. Normally you would only attempt power with the simpler shots since the technique required tends to weaken the control you usually have over your cueing action. The chance of errors creeping in is therefore made that much greater.

Once you understand the reason for playing a power shot, you will tend to be more selective in your choice of that shot. Basically it is used to gain you position that you would otherwise not achieve by playing at normal pace. It may look impressive to see the cue ball flashing round the table or to hear that object ball crash into a pocket, but the consequences can be disastrous.

The principle to remember is that you should hit the cue ball with the minimum degree of pace to achieve the maximum run after contact for position on the next shot. How much pace you require will depend on the circumstances. The other value of a power shot is that you can, as Jimmy puts it, 'steal an angle'. This is possible because your cue action is forcing the ball through at speed and you do not need to strike the object ball directly into the centre of the pocket. With the pace that is generated, it should whip in off the jaws, allowing you to angle the shot slightly.

It is easy to assume, when you watch someone like Jimmy, that all he is doing is smashing the cue ball across the table. This isn't true. Of course he is

hitting the ball harder, but the action involved is still very much controlled and the power comes basically from the timing of the shot.

To achieve extra power you must lengthen your back swing, which means lengthening your cue grip to suit. For maximum power, you would use the butt-end grip, with your little finger wrapped round the butt. In this case you bring the tip of your cue back as far as you can to the 'V' of your bridged hand without losing control over it. You then bring the cue forward into the strike with the required pace, keeping the rest of your body as still as possible.

The temptation is to put as much force into the shot as you can through your body, but this will only cause movement in the shot, particularly lifting the head. And as the head goes up, so will the cue. You must keep as low as possible, with your head firmly down – and kept down. The extra length of back swing will generate more pace, while you must concentrate on a smooth delivery and not snatch or dig at the cue ball.

You will need power for a screw shot, as already described, but the pace will depend on the distance between the cue ball and object ball. A perfect example of controlled power in this situation is Jimmy. I have seen him literally stroke a screw shot, when the object ball has only just reached the pocket, and then all of a sudden the cue ball has started rolling back.

There seems to be a great tendency to play power shots in the amateur game. I remember in those earlier days I used to be one of the most powerful players around and could produce really deep screw shots. It may not have mattered too much then scattering balls all round the table. But I quickly learnt the error of my ways when I joined the professional ranks, since if you do that you often don't get another shot for the rest of the frame!

If I get the shot right, I can screw back up to 15 ft. with the cue ball. But now I really only attempt to do this when going for safety off a long pot, when I want to bring the cue ball back to baulk. Jimmy, as I said, is another very powerful player and the secret seems to be in the whip of the arm. Some players have this, others don't. There again, it also depends on the condition of the table. You cannot achieve that length of screw back if the table is playing slowly.

Of the Matchroom players, Tony is also quite

To play the power shot, you need to lengthen your back swing. You can see clearly here how much further back the right arm comes for a power shot in comparison to that of medium pace. Notice too how the line of the knuckles changes and the right arm drops slightly to achieve the extra length. If you check back with the section on Striking the ball, you can see how this action differs from the normal cueing action.

---

powerful, as is Terry when he uses it. Steve has also got the power, but you will rarely see him play a deep screw shot. It is certainly a shot you should try to develop into your game if you can, but one you should usually keep back for that emergency, when you need to get yourself out of trouble and there is no other route to take. Of course, there will be occasions when a shot like that could prove a frame or match winner and then you will have to decide how you feel at the time. But normally it is a shot to be used as a last resort.

Having said that, I pulled out one of my best screw shots ever against John Virgo in the 1986 Embassy World Championships. In fact it won me the shot of the tournament award. I went for a long red and must have screwed the cue ball back all of 10 ft. It was the first pot of the frame and the reds were everywhere. If I had missed it I would have been in big trouble. As it was, I went on to make over 70 and take the frame.

I think without doubt the best shot I have ever played was when I beat Cliff Thorburn in the final of the BCE in 1986. Again it was a long screw shot, but what impressed me was that the cue ball was only 6 in. from the cushion and the shot was made twice as hard because I was bridging over the rail. Instead of getting really low, I was having to cue down, which makes it much more difficult to get the right power into the shot. But I played it – and it came off.

THE SWERVE

Although you may be tempted to take on the swerve shot when there is an easy pot, with the object ball hanging near the pocket, but there is another ball fractionally in your path, normally this type of shot is played to get out of a snooker. Personally I would only play it when there was no other shot on or if I didn't have a reasonably easy escape off one or two cushions. Equally I would avoid it if I had to swerve more than a ball's width or get round more than one ball.

The principle behind the swerve shot is to play it wide of the obstructing ball but with sufficient side to bring it back on line to hit the object ball. To do this, you have to apply extreme top side, which means lifting the butt of the cue and striking down on to the cue ball. This has the effect of making the ball bounce along the cloth slightly. When it stops bouncing it can grip the cloth and the side takes effect. Having said that, you can appreciate the problems involved and the possibility for error.

The width of the arc will depend on the amount of side you apply and the length of the arc on the pace of the cue ball. The slower you play the shot, the earlier the side will take effect and bring the cue ball back – when the obstructing ball is closer to you. The further away it is, the more pace you need in the shot, so that the cue ball 'bends' back later.

The side you put on will be the opposite to the way you are sending the cue ball. So if you are playing to the left of the obstructing ball, you would use right-hand side – and, of course, left-hand side when playing to the right.

These are useful shots to be able to play, but they are also quite hard to judge. It is all a question of feel and accurate striking – and a degree of luck as well. I say this, because you can never guarantee exactly the amount of swerve you will get on the ball, particularly if you are playing on a strange table.

Oddly enough, you often find you can play this shot better on a club table than one of our tournament tables. Although our tables are more lively, there is not always so much grip in the cloth – it's usually more silky. Imagine what is happening to the ball. You push it out to one side and then have to wait until it grips and swerves back in again. Where exactly it grips is therefore very important in judging the shot.

I remember having to play this shot against Dennis in the 1987 Embassy World Championships. There was no way round the cushions and I really had to dig into the shot. I had to swerve the ball 4 or 5 in. to the right, which really is too much for me, and I ended up missing it by just a fraction of an inch. You can never tell.

The extreme type of swerve shot is a massé, where you literally hit down from virtually on top of the cue

The swerve shot does provide a solution to getting out of a snooker, provided there is room to play the cue ball round the obstructing ball. This is always a risky shot, since you need to judge the distances carefully and will have to play down on the cue ball, applying top spin as well as side, to take it round the first ball and then back on line to hit the object ball. The safer way of playing a snooker is off the cushions.

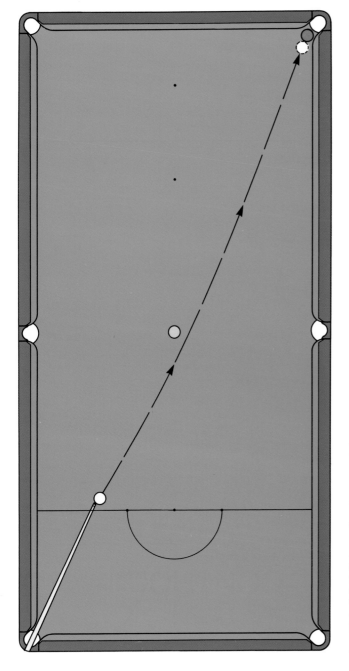

Above: The massé is an extreme swerve shot where you are applying maximum top spin by literally hitting down on top of the cue ball. The shot is a very risky one and is really only played where the cue ball, obstructing ball and object ball are very close to one another – and when there is really no other option left open to you.

Left: When playing a swerve shot, you must remember that you need to play the cue ball with opposite side to that which you want to send the ball round the obstructing ball. So if you want to play to the right of this ball, then you will have to use left-hand side. The width of the arc on which the cue ball travels will depend on how much side you apply and the length of the arc on the pace of the shot.

ball. You very rarely see this played nowadays and, of course, it is a specialised shot for special situations, where the cue ball, obstructing ball and object ball are all very close to one another. What you are achieving is a complete U-turn of the cue ball using extreme top and side spin.

Although the swerve can be a very satisfying and effective shot to play, I would always recommend you look for all possible alternatives before taking it on. As far as I'm concerned, there are too many risks involved with no final guarantee that the shot will work the way you want.

COMBINATION SHOTS

BY DENNIS TAYLOR

There are basically two types of combination shot – the plant and the double. Neither is particularly easy to play since in each case you are not attempting to play the object ball direct into the pocket. But they are worth practising because they can well be frame-winners – and certainly enable you to continue a break when it looks as though all is lost.

THE PLANT

A straightforward plant is where you have two reds close to each other and directly in line with a pocket. In this situation, all you have to do is aim as if you were potting the first red. Provided you line up this correctly it will knock the second red in.

The problems come when the two reds are touching or just a fraction apart. Although they may be in direct line with the pocket, as before, if you hit the first red in the normal way you will in fact 'squeeze' the second red slightly off course and will almost certainly miss the pocket. The secret is not to get too thick a contact on the first red – preferably no more than half-ball. If the angle is fuller, then you should play to strike it on the thin side. For the less time the two reds are in contact with each other, the less chance there is of the first interfering with the second.

The effect this can have is best explained in the illustration. But you actually need to strike the first red fractionally on the opposite side. For the reaction between the balls is in fact opposite to what most people would think. If you strike the object ball on the right-hand side, it will push the second red to the left.

This is best demonstrated when you have two reds in a plant but slightly off line with the pocket. Unless you were aware of how touching balls can react, you would probably look at it and say there was no way of potting the second red. In fact there is, but you have to make sure you strike the first red on the correct side. Most would assume that if the reds are lined up to the left of the pocket, you would have to make contact with the right-hand side of the first red to push the second red to the right, ie trying to play the first ball across the second. This is wrong. You need to hit the object ball on the left to push the second red to the right.

The best way to see how balls react in a plant situation is to set them up in different ways and experiment. Play the plant first with the balls touching and then with them $\frac{1}{4}$, $\frac{1}{2}$ and 1 in. apart. Judgement here is of course critical since there is no margin for error. Contact with the object ball has to be spot on.

The first occasion you are likely to have in a frame to play a plant would be early in the game when the cluster of reds has not been split. Possibly your opponent has played a safety shot bringing the cue ball back down into the baulk area. Now normally the tactics would be to reply with a similar safety shot. But it is worth having a look at the pack to see if there is a possible plant on – it could even be three or four-ball – into one of the top pockets. The person who is likely to seize the advantage is the one who spots a possible plant first and plays it successfully, rather than matching safety with safety.

Obviously a plant in this situation does carry an element of risk. But you can reduce this by playing it in such a way as to bring the cue ball back towards the baulk end. If you do get the pot, then you are on one of the baulk colours. If you miss it, you have at least left the cue ball relatively safe. You can, of course, play for position on the black or pink, but this carries greater dangers should you miss the pot.

Generally during a frame the plant will be much more obvious, where you have a couple of reds close to each other in line with a pocket. As long as you know how to play them, there should be little risk in this situation.

Interestingly, it was the Canadians who started playing the plant as a regular part of their game. Cliff Thorburn and Bill Werbenuik are the best examples. But nowadays we are all looking for them – and Jimmy is particularly strong here, sometimes picking out quite complicated three or four-ball plants.

There is a tip for those who find it difficult to line a plant up accurately where the two reds are, say, a couple of inches off line and slightly apart. When you have decided where to make contact on the first red, follow this imaginary line through to the cushion and concentrate on the spot you need to knock the first red on to when playing the shot. You must forget the second red, otherwise you can lose concentration on the first ball by trying to take in both balls at once. Provided you have lined the plant up and you strike the first red correctly, the second will go in.

The basic plant is where you have two reds near each other and in line with the pocket. In this situation the reds are in fact touching and you would have to play what we call a 'squeeze' shot. The way this is done is clearly explained in the illustration, but involves making thinner contact with the first red.

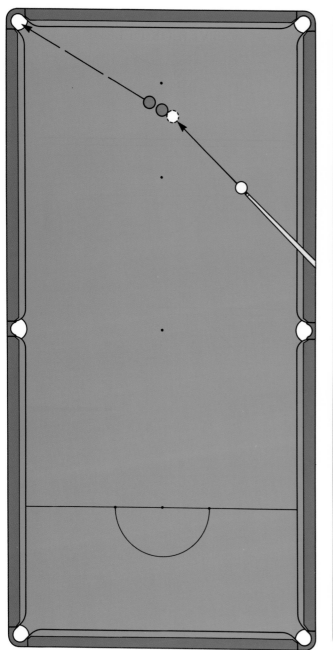

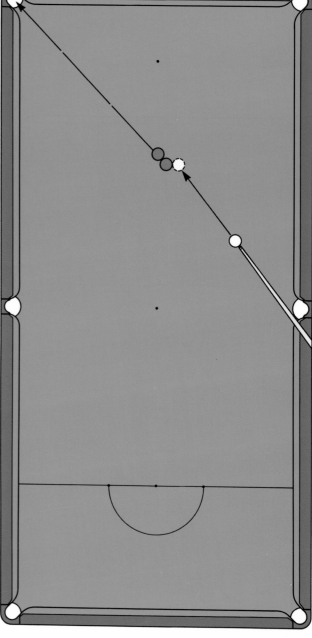

This shows clearly the basic plant situation, where the reds are directly in line with the pocket. It doesn't matter where the cue ball is, since by using the right potting angle for the first red, you should pot the second. This only applies when the balls are close to each other, not when they are touching.

When the balls are touching or just a fraction apart, you have what is known as a 'squeeze' shot. If you strike the first red in the normal way it will in effect squeeze the second red off line. To allow for this you must make thinner contact with the first red — no more than a half-ball — which should then send the second red into the pocket.

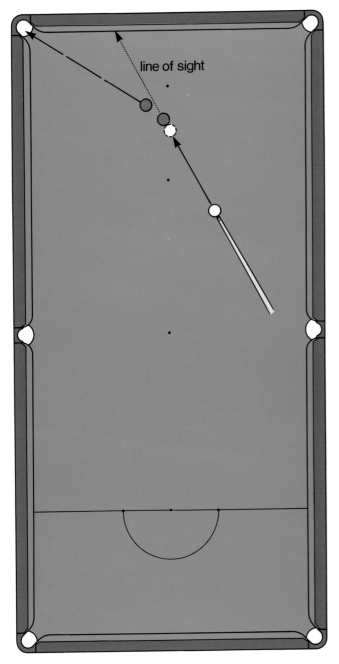

line of sight

It is possible to play a plant when there are two reds close to each other but slightly off line with the pocket. First you should establish what contact you need on the first red to pot the second. Having done this, you will find it easier to follow this line of sight from the cue ball through the first red and on to the cushion. By concentrating on this spot on the cushion when playing the shot, you will not be distracted by the second red and should make the pot.

THE DOUBLE

The double involves playing the object ball off the cushion into the pocket opposite, which already means there is an element of risk in the shot, since you must get the angles absolutely right. People often ask why we as professionals don't play doubles. That is not strictly true. But we tend only to play them when we really have to and then normally it's a percentage shot – where the chances of getting it are reasonable under the circumstances, but we are not leaving too much on if we should miss.

The problem with the double is, as I said, in judging the angles correctly. If you get this slightly wrong the ball can go anywhere, probably leaving your opponent in. It is a tough shot to judge because you must know the cushions and how they react, since they can all play differently. What you have to do is ensure the object ball comes off the cushion at the right angle and that only comes with practice.

The easiest is where you are aiming for a 45 degree angle, since struck correctly the object ball will then come off at the same angle you were aiming for. But sometimes a full-ball direct won't get you the double and you need instead a threequarter or half-ball. The angle the ball comes off will also depend on how hard it is struck. The harder you play the shot, the squarer the object ball will come off, as it digs itself into the cushion.

I should mention here that there are three other types of double. Apart from the basic full-ball, there is the cross double, the cut-back double and the 'cocked hat'.

With the cross double, you play the cue ball across the face of the object ball before it doubles over the table. The cut-back double is the opposite of this shot, where you are aiming the cue ball to the far side of the object ball. The 'cocked hat' is by far the hardest to judge, since this involves sending the object ball off three cushions. You can see how each of these work from the illustrations.

Normally the only time you see people playing doubles is when attempting to pot into the middle pocket, although you can use this technique into the top or bottom pockets as well.

Those who can play doubles well are usually good at billiards, which I used to play a lot when I was younger. I would certainly recommend anyone to

This is the standard double situation, where you are aiming to play the object ball off the cushion and back across the table into the middle pocket. There is of course always an element of risk in this shot, since you need to get the angle absolutely right.

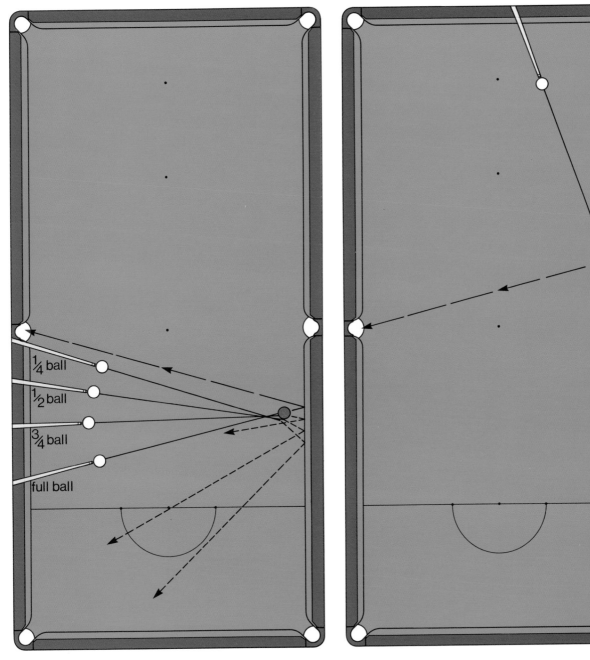

¼ ball

½ ball

¾ ball

full ball

Here you can see how the angle for the double affects the path of the cue ball after contact with the object ball. With a full-ball shot, the cue ball will travel in the same direction as the object ball. The thinner the contact, the more the cue ball will run back down the table. The angles shown here represent a cut-back double. For a normal double the cue ball would run on up the table. One important point to bear in mind when you are playing the double is that the harder you strike the cue ball the squarer the angle at which it will come off the cushion.

This illustration shows the cross double. Here you are playing the cue ball across the face of the object ball. In this situation the cue ball will run on down the table before the object ball doubles back off the cushion into the pocket.

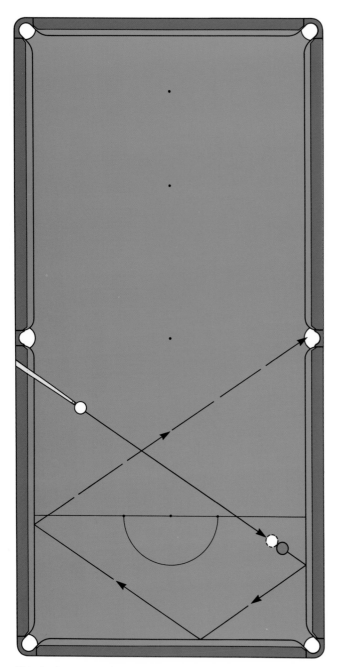

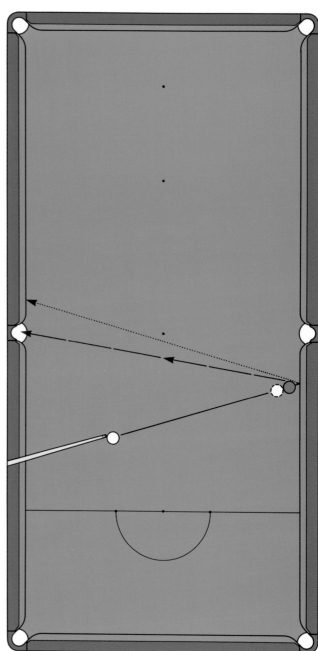

This is the most difficult of all the doubles. Known as the cocked hat double, for obvious reasons, it involves sending the object ball off three cushions and into the pocket. Because of the accuracy required for the angles, it is a shot that is rarely played.

This is an interesting variation on the double and in fact was a shot I played against Cliff Thorburn in the 1986 Hong Kong Masters. There were two problems I had to overcome. One was the danger of getting a double kiss and the other that by playing a normal shot I would miss the middle pocket (as indicated by the dotted line). The solution was to put bottom on the cue ball to stun it on contact with the black and also left-hand side to square the black up as it came off the cushion. It worked and the black went in.

practise this way, since you will find it much easier to understand and get used to angles, particularly when playing for cannons. Just sending the cue ball round the table off the cushions will help you judge how these work.

You can also set up a billiards situation on the snooker table with three balls and try playing cannons to see how the balls react on contact. Having played plain-ball, you can then experiment with left and right-hand side and see what effect this has when the ball comes off the cushion.

In general, combination shots are the kind that you would probably only use in practice, to start with anyway. You have to know what is going to happen before you try them on in a match. And even then you should avoid any reckless shots. It's basically down to assessing the situation on the table and playing to percentages. There's always a right and a wrong time to play a shot. Unfortunately the wrong time can prove very costly.

TACTICAL PLAY

INTRODUCTION BY STEVE DAVIS

What snooker fan will ever forget the final of the 1985 Embassy World Championship between Dennis Taylor and myself? What snooker fan will ever forget that Dennis was 8–0 down and came back to win on the black in the deciding frame? I certainly won't!

The final of the world championship – as with most other major tournaments – is usually played between the two most in-form players in those two weeks. Sometimes the only thing separating them at this stage is their tactical ability. All other aspects of their play – potting, positioning, etc – are taken for granted. Then the margin between victory and defeat rests on who eventually gains tactical supremacy – and this is probably Dennis's greatest strength.

Not only has he got a sound all-round game, but he is able to strike that special balance between attack and defence. It is like a sixth sense – an instinctive ability to know just when to go for a shot and when to play safe or close up the game.

In present day terms, it took Dennis a long time to reach the very top, despite being one of the most established players over the last two decades. One reason was the problems he had with his glasses, now successfully and spectacularly overcome. Another reason I believe was that he hadn't got his tactical game exactly right. As soon as he did, the rest fell into place and he gained enormous confidence.

As I said, nobody can make you into a good tactical player. But it is, in my opinion, one of the greatest compliments you can be paid as a player. There is no worse a feeling than to lose a match through stupid shots. There is nothing embarrassing about missing a pot. It happens to the best of players. But it is embarrassing to have misread the score or played a shot that has left your opponent in for an easy clearance or given away a free ball from which he can win the match.

At the top level of the game, tactical play probably accounts for half the matches won or lost. The other half reflects general all-round ability at the time. In terms of club handicaps, you would need somebody who was 28 points worse than yourself to guarantee beating him on level terms, because you would know he was a weaker player. If you were to play somebody just seven points worse than you, then the only difference would probably be in the tactical approach to the game.

The importance of thinking tactically in a match is best highlighted by the approach you should be adopting in a competitive situation. All the time you are practising, you are concentrating solely on technique – on getting your shots right. When you enter a match, your whole train of thought should be about the way the game is going, what tactics to adopt, whether the shot is the right one to play or not.

I suppose it is natural to assume that tactical players are generally slower players. That, of course, is not necessarily true although the person who takes more time between shots is usually considered to be more of a thinker. But this process need not always be to a player's advantage. I do believe that there are times in a match when you need to rely on instinct, while on other occasions you must be guided by your brain. It is this fine balance that separates players on a tactical level.

In this final section on tactical play, Dennis looks at matchplay and the various aspects of safety required in different situations. In offering tactical hints and general guiding principles, he is helping you to assess for yourself how best to respond to different experiences at a competitive level.

As you play more snooker, more competitions and tournaments, whether at club level or higher, you will gradually build up not just a repertoire of shots you either like or dislike, but also a series of experiences of situations that you have benefitted from or found dangerous and costly. These you have to learn to store away and remember the next time a similar situation occurs. Usually you will find your subconscious recalls what you did the last time and if it went wrong you may try something different.

I stressed the importance in Planning Shots of being adaptable and this applies just as much in your tactical approach to the game. You musn't go into a match or a frame, for that matter, with fixed thoughts in your head of how you are going to play, whether to attack or play safe. You must play the balls on the table as you find them. Remember, you are not playing against a person; you are playing against the table. When you return to the table after your opponent's last shot, the balls will be in a different position and you must play them accordingly. If you can think of it in those terms, you are far less likely to be put off by your opponent, whoever he is – even Dennis!

TACTICAL PLAY

BY DENNIS TAYLOR

Having the ability to play the game of snooker well doesn't ever guarantee results. Although you may have studied the various sections of this book and feel that you have to some degree mastered the techniques necessary to play a full range of shots, the difference between winning and losing can often be a question of tactics.

Every match you play – indeed, every frame – sets up different situations, all requiring on-the-spot decisions. Should I attack or defend? Do I go for a pot or play safe? These and many more questions have to be answered umpteen times during a match and how you do it will more often than not effect the final result. It can mean losing when you're playing well and winning when you're not. Your mental approach is, of course, a critical factor too, but tactics are very much part of the experience you gain from playing competition snooker.

THE BREAK-OFF

This is, of course, the very first shot of every frame and how you play it can have a psychological effect on how the game goes from there. A good break-off shot can put immediate pressure on your opponent. Equally a bad one can lose you the frame.

To prove to you how crucial this shot can be – not only for the frame but also the match – I need look no further than an incident that happened to me quite recently in a tournament. I was playing Martin Clark, an 18-year-old. It was his first match in front of the television cameras, so he was already under some pressure and I needed a good start to prevent him from settling.

I won the toss and broke off, hoping to put the pressure on from the first shot. I made a complete hash of it by hitting the blue and left him a reasonable pot which he got. He went on to make a 20-odd break and that relaxed him. Having settled in from the word go, he went from strength to strength and beat me 5–0. That one careless shot seemed to have affected the pattern of the entire match.

So this should provide an object lesson in how essential it is to practise a good opening shot. And there are several ways of doing this, as you will see if you watch the different professionals. Most players will aim for the end red using some right-hand side on the cue ball to bring it off the top and side cushion

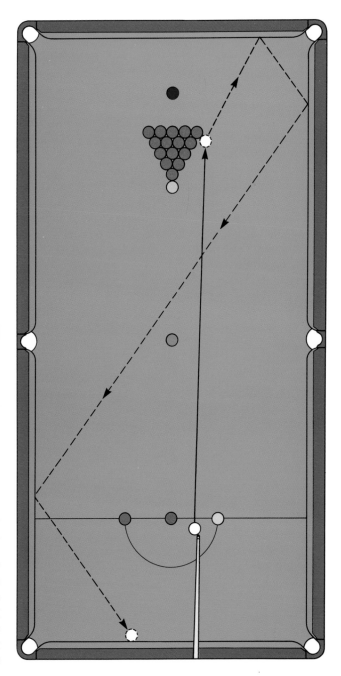

The idea with the break-off shot is to disturb the pack of reds as little as possible and bring the cue ball back down the table as near to the baulk cushon as possible. The normal shot, which most professionals play, is to play the cue ball from between the yellow and green using left-hand side and aiming to strike the last red in the pack. The cue ball should then travel off the top and side cushions, back between the pink and blue and into baulk via the other side cushion.

and back in between the pink and blue towards baulk. This shot doesn't split the reds too much – at most moving three or four of them.

The ideal place to leave the cue ball is tight against the bottom cushion. Sometimes you will see a player tuck the cue ball up against the green, for example, which is fine if you can put it there, but I would always recommend the bottom cushion in preference.

The reason, which I shall talk about in more detail later, is that in this situation your opponent has to cue awkwardly and play the length of the table, hopefully with enough power to bring the cue ball back to the bottom again, which is very difficult. With a snooker behind the green, all he need do is play a soft shot off the side cushion into the pack of reds, which is a fair-sized target.

While the vast majority play the cue ball from between the brown and yellow, the exact position does vary. Jimmy, for example, cues off from very close to the yellow and normally aims for the second to last red – and sometimes even the third to last. He does this to give himself more of an angle to avoid the in-off into the top right-hand pocket, which is another common problem for beginners after they have learnt to miss the blue! A tip here is that the thicker the contact, the less likely you are to go in-off.

The danger of striking this part of the pack is that you do tend to spread the balls a lot more. Jimmy's thoughts here are to tempt his opponent into taking a long red, which if he misses lets Jimmy straight in with plenty of reds to go for. But of course if Jimmy fails to bring the cue ball back to baulk and it gets trapped at the top end, he leaves his opponent well in for a big break. So it's a great attacking break if you play the shot right, but there is a lot more risk involved, too.

You will see a few players breaking off from the other side of the brown – that is, in between the brown and the green. The only difference here is that you use left-hand side rather than right on the cue ball. But either way you are aiming to bring the cue ball back off three cushions. In the olden days players would play a plain ball, clipping the reds and running the cue ball off two cushions back to baulk. The problem here was that there was more chance of striking a baulk colour on the way back down and leaving the cue ball in a more playable position.

SAFETY PLAY

The tactical battle really begins after the break-off and your approach to shots will obviously depend on how the balls lie after the pack of reds has been split. Although it is always a good feeling to get points on the board, you should never rush in and go for the slightest chance. For one reason, at the start of a frame – and particularly the first frame – you cannot possibly have got into any sort of rhythm, which reduces the chances of getting a tough pot.

It is far better to start cautiously and build your game up as the chances come. For the early tactical battle is the one you should always aim to win to give you an advantage over your opponent. This is why you see people playing a series of safety shots until they are given a good opening.

Steve is often described as a slowish player, but that's not strictly fair. He certainly won't take any risks early on because he realises the importance of winning that first frame and getting off to a good start. That's why, when people like Steve and I play each other, the safety play may go on a little longer at the beginning of a frame. We are both pretty strong in this department and each is waiting to force an error from the other.

This is one of Steve's many qualities. He has the ability to play safe for quite some time but still take the chance to knock the balls in when it occurs. Few players can do that. After playing a long period of safety, they lose their rhythm and fluff the opportunity.

Once you start potting a few balls and get into a rhythm, then you can think about taking on more risky shots. But there are other factors, such as how you feel on the day and whether you are confident with your technique. Some days you will be potting well, while on other days nothing seems to go in.

I shall never forget what the great Joe Davis once said to me: "You are never going to become a better potter. The way you are going to improve is to eliminate shots from your game." In other words, you have to think about and decide on percentages. When you are faced with a shot that you would normally get only three or four times out of ten, then you should leave it alone. If it is one that you would normally expect to get six or seven times out of ten, then you can have a go at it.

The secret is to work out and recognise your weaknesses and concentrate on playing to your strengths, particularly when you are not feeling on top form. And if you are not sure, then play safe.

I have built up quite a reputation for making things difficult for my opponent. It is not that I am a defensive player by nature, but I am quite happy to play a tactical game and vary my safety to suit. In fact as an amateur I learnt to play the sort of shots you would have seen from John Spencer and now see from Jimmy. I could screw back the full length of the table and used to enjoy playing to please the crowd. But then my opponent would step in, playing a careful tactical game, and I found I was on the losing end all the time.

It depends to a great extent on whom you are playing as to how you work out the game. I love playing against Jimmy or Stephen Hendry, because you would normally expect to be given more chances. When you are up against people like Steve, Terry or Cliff Thorburn, you know you are in for a real tactical struggle until the balls open up and give the chance of a high break. We can all build the big breaks when the opportunity arises, but sometimes you have to out-wit the opposition first.

Of course there are different ways of playing safety and you should vary the type of shots you use depending on your opponent. If he is an attacking

player, it is often a good idea to play safe in such a way as to leave him a half-chance, rather than put him in dead trouble. He will probably be tempted to have a go at it and, if he gets it, all well and good. But you were playing to the percentages; if he missed, then you were in.

I used to play this way against Perrie Mans, who was renowned as an out-and-out potter of the ball, but was not as good at positional or safety play. Instead of trying to put him in real trouble with a telling safety shot, I would leave him in such a position that he had the half-chance of a pot, knowing that he would take it on.

To play a good safety shot can sometimes be just as difficult as taking on a hard pot. But you are also minimising the risks and it is certainly an essential part of anyone's game, if they want to win tournaments.

An example of this is the classic safety shot where you are bringing the cue ball back into baulk, having clipped an object ball at the top end of the table. When you leave the cue ball in front of the 'D', this is classed as a poor safety shot, since ideally you want to tuck it up by the bottom cushion. But in fairness you have to consider that you are making the cue ball travel up to 24 feet to get into that position, which requires great judgement and precision.

PRACTICE
CLIPPING THE OBJECT BALLS

You will find this exercise helps you play those awkward long shots where you just want to touch the object ball and bring the cue ball back safely into baulk.

Place a few balls near the top cushion and the cue ball anywhere in the 'D'. Then practise playing up the table, just clipping each of the object balls in turn and bringing the cue ball back down the table. You can vary this by bringing the cue ball further back behind the baulk line until you are playing it off the bottom cushion.

This exercise helps you judge the contact you need on the object ball, since you must get as thin a contact as possible, while of course controlling the pace of the shot as well.

ATTACK OR DEFEND?

There are times when it is very difficult to play a safety shot. Then you have to weigh up in your own mind exactly how to go about it. The option is to take on an equally difficult pot and you can only decide on the basis of how you feel at the time. If you are potting well and feeling confident, then you should go for the ball.

That happened to me in the 1985 World Championship when I played Steve in that memorable final. I was faced with a very difficult brown. The alternative was to play safe which, had I messed it up, would have let Steve in – and I would never have forgiven myself for losing that way. I went for pot.

So there are occasions when you will opt for the difficult pot. Equally, if it is a straightforward safety shot, then you will play that.

You learn through experience where you have gone all out with your shots and paid the penalty. If you are going well, then you will usually take on the tough pots. You must apply a degree of discipline and self-control, however, and be able to assess each situation as it occurs.

I have to admit – and we all do it – that there are times when I will go for a shot I know I shouldn't. I admit that goes against everything I have learnt and experienced. But that's what makes snooker such a fascinating game. We can all come up with the unexpected. At least it proves we're all human, too.

MOVING THE BALLS

Another very important part of safety play is knowing when to move balls into or out of commission, depending on the state of the game. If you are putting your opponent under pressure, you want to make sure that when he lets you in you do have a chance at the colours. Equally, when you are on the receiving end, you can upset his break by ensuring, for example, the high colours are on or near the cushions.

A few examples will help illustrate this. You have just potted a red into one of the top pockets and there are no colours on. You have decided to take the cue ball to the baulk end, but the black is tied up on the side cushion. As you are playing safe and leaving your opponent nothing, you could play the black off the cushion as you send the cue ball down the other end. If you put him in trouble and he leaves you on, having potted a red you then have the black back in commission.

The reverse situation would be where you were up against an opponent like Jimmy who was knocking in everything and you just couldn't get in. Then you would try to put the black, for example, on to the side cushion to restrict the colours he could go for until you got your rhythm back. The principle here is that if you can't get your game going then you need to interrupt that of your opponent, otherwise he will pot you off the table. Sometimes it is just a question of giving yourself more time at the table to get your cue working properly.

It all depends on how the match is going at the time. But you need to appreciate that some players can be off form and still win because of their tactical play, while if an out-and-out potter finds things are

not going right for him he can easily lose out of sheer frustration.

Another aspect of this that is important is being able to keep the score in your head all the time. Particularly when you are in front, you need to know what is left on the table. Having worked out, for example, that your opponent needs three reds and three blacks, plus the colours, to win, you can make things very awkward by pushing the black on to the cushion.

Equally you may be trailing by quite some way. You can at least interrupt your opponent's flow by knocking a colour against a cushion which means he will need more than one visit to the table to win the frame.

You are ahead in the frame and have just potted a red. Unfortunately there is no colour on and the break has come to an end. Instead of playing a straightforward safety shot, you should take the opportunity of pushing a colour on to the side to make life even harder and improve your chances of winning that frame.

By the same token, if you know there are enough loose balls on the table for you to win the frame, then there is no point in bringing any awkward balls out into play. The danger here is that should you break down, then your opponent can take advantage of the fact that you have released more colours for him to pot. Your primary concern should be to make a big enough break to win.

In all this safety play, a knowledge of angles is very important. That is one of the reasons why I have a good safety game – as does Steve – because we can use side to clip off the object ball and swing the cue ball round the cushions.

SHOT TO NOTHING

This is basically where you are faced with a difficult pot, but in playing it you are running the cue ball into a relatively safe position so that should you miss the shot you will not leave your opponent in.

This type of shot is normally played around the top of the table, where you have an escape route to the baulk end. If the pot does go in, then at least you are on a baulk colour to keep the break going. The only possible way you could leave the shot is if the object ball ends up right near the pocket without going in. But then there is still the chance that you have snookered your opponent behind one of the baulk colours.

One great advantage of a shot to nothing is that you can play it even when your game is not going very well, because of the safety element. And if you do get the pot it will probably boost your confidence, with the result that your play improves, too.

Fred Davis was a great exponent of the shot to nothing and he would do it in situations where you would have thought he was taking enormous risks. One particular time he used this was with the reds scattered around the top of the table. He would play a pot into the middle pocket and get position on the black for the next shot. You would have thought that, if he missed it, his opponent could pick out one of the other reds easily. But Fred made sure that although he was on the black, it was impossible to pot any of the other reds. It was a very clever shot.

PLAYING SNOOKERS

Snookers can be a very effective weapon in tactical play, but you do need to know when to play them, since they can actually present the advantage to your opponent. Sometimes, of course, they are necessary for winning the frame, if you are trailing and there aren't enough points on the table.

During a game, the most common place to effect a snooker is by running the cue ball up behind one of the baulk colours. A good example of this is following a shot to nothing, where you have made the pot, the rest of the reds are well spread but you have left yourself in an awkward position to pot another colour. Then probably your best shot is to roll the cue ball behind one of the baulk colours to snooker your opponent.

By taking on a difficult pot, you are putting unnecessary pressure on yourself. By tucking the cue ball up, you are forcing your opponent to negotiate the snooker and get the ball safe. He may achieve the first objective. But with the reds well spread, he is more than likely to leave you up for your next shot.

A bad time to play the snooker is when the reds are tightly clustered, as I mentioned earlier with the break-off. This is quite a simple situation to get out

of, since all your opponent has to do is run the cue ball off a side cushion into the pack, leaving you with no advantage.

I remember seeing Steve play a very good attacking safety shot in a similar situation. Instead of running the cue ball up behind one of the baulk colours, he played it into the pack to split the reds and screwed it back into the baulk area.

A further situation is worth mentioning where one side of the pack of reds has been opened out, while the other side is still tightly packed. When you are tucking the cue ball up behind a colour, make sure you do so in such a way as to block off the path to the tight side of the pack. This means that your opponent has to play into the scattered reds to get out of the snooker, which gives you a much better chance of being left on with your next shot.

GETTING OUT OF SNOOKERS

Having discussed how to set a snooker, the boot could be on the other foot and you therefore need to practise how to get out of one. This means working at your angles, since you cannot play a direct shot on to the object ball. Your only other option is to swerve the cue ball, which has already been discussed. Some players prefer to play a snooker this way and I will use that shot sometimes.

There is always a degree of luck involved in getting out of a snooker, because however well you work out the angles, you can never guarantee exactly the angle at which the cue ball will come off or where exactly on the object ball it will strike. Final position on the cue ball is even harder to estimate. You would, of course, try in some cases to hit it on one side or another to ensure the cue ball runs on – hopefully back to safety.

There is one golden rule, however, when playing to get out of a snooker. You should never miss the object ball and end up leaving a free ball. This is particularly important if you are ahead in the frame and your opponent needs snookers to overhaul you. Although you will give away points if you miss the object ball, this does not necessarily give him any positional advantage. But a free ball certainly will. And if he doesn't opt to take it, it means you have to play the next shot as well.

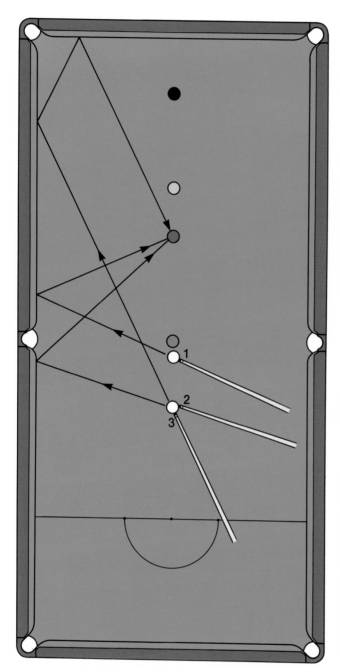

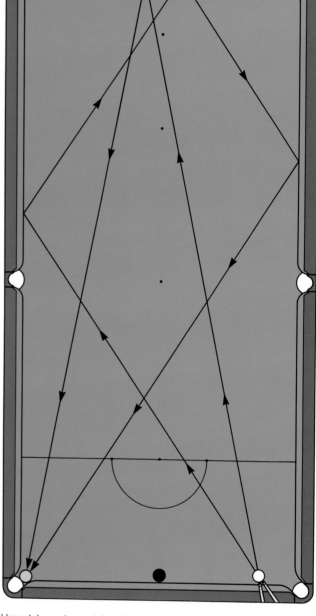

The problem here, as you can see, is that I am snookered on the brown. With shot 1 the solution is a straightforward double off the side cushion. The problem I have with the cue ball further down the table is that I cannot use the normal double since the middle pocket is in the way. I therefore have two choices. With shot 2 I can play the double, but will need to use right-hand side to widen the angle at which the cue ball comes off the cushion, aiming just below the pocket. The alternative, with shot 3, is to play off two cushions and bring the cue ball back down the table.

Here I have been left with an awkward snooker on the baulk cushion. The one advantage I do have is that the pink is right over the pocket, but I will need to get my angles right in order to hit it. The simpler shot is to play the cue ball right up the table, off the top cushion and back to the pink. Alternatively I can play the cue ball off three cushions and in this case would probably use a little right-hand side on the ball.

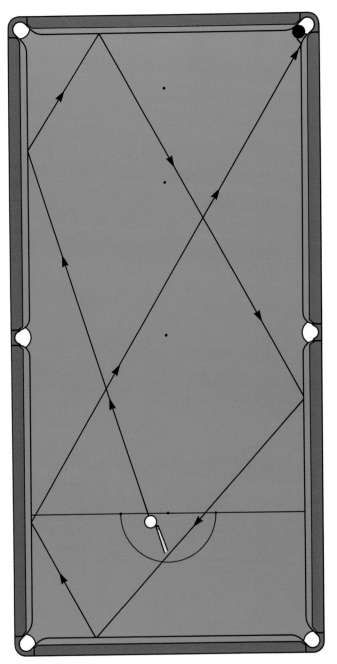

This is one way of practising the angles using as many cushions as possible. Here I am in fact playing the cue ball off six cushions to try and pot the object ball, using a little right-hand side on the cue ball. You can set up what situation you like, but the important thing is to watch the angles at which the cue ball comes off each cushion and try to remember these. At first you can only see how close you get to the object ball. If you do finally pot it, then snookers shouldn't be a problem again!

PRACTICE

USING THE ANGLES

There are two stages to this practice, which is basically for helping you to use the cushions to get out of a snooker.

First play with the cue ball alone and send it around the cushions towards a nominated pocket. Check the angles as you play and see how close you can get the cue ball to your chosen pocket.

Now put another ball on the table and continue the exercise using as many cushions as possible and see how near to the object ball you can get the cue ball. What you are aiming to achieve is to be able to make contact with the object ball as much as possible. If you can do this everytime, you need never worry about a snooker again!

MATCHPLAY

This is the true test of a snooker player. You may be able to do marvellous things on the practice table and in the club, but tournament conditions are very different indeed. So many aspects are important, not least of which are temperament and control over your game – when to attack and when to play safe, as I have already talked about.

Most amateurs when they turn professional need to work hard on their safety play and tactics. They have been used to playing with others who use a similar attacking style, but the professional game can be very different. Obviously they can all pot balls and make 100 breaks. But then their lack of safety lets them down.

As far as temperament is concerned, you need to be able to cope with all situations. You may have just made a complete hash of a shot – or, worse still, – you just can't get your game going. In the meantime, you just have to sit it out and watch your opponent take over at the table.

I have talked about the various ways in which you can try to play yourself back into a game – using safety shots, upsetting your opponent's rhythm by making it difficult for him to pot balls and so on. When you have played a poor or rash shot and let him back in, you must never sit and brood about it.

By the time you get back to the table you must have put it out of your mind so that you can start afresh. Of course, that is easier said than done.

Temperament plays such an important part of the game, but unfortunately it is not something you can be taught. It is a natural gift – or fault, whichever way you look at it. Either you have a good temperament or you haven't. But if you do suffer from poor temperament in match situations, then you have got to try to work on it and at least control it.

You can help with this by overcoming those blunders that are probably costing you the match. When you have missed a shot, don't keep going through it in your mind, since when you get back to the table you will only do the same again. You can't practise it while the match is on, so put it to one side and go back to it later. The chances are that you will be faced with a similar shot again and you have got to go straight into it as if you have never missed it. Otherwise you will talk yourself out of it quite easily.

This highlights another golden rule. Apart from possibly a minor adjustment here or there, never be tempted to change your technique during a match. The place to do that is on the practice table back at the club. If you start worrying about the basics at that stage, you will simply go from bad to worse.

Preparing for a match is really down to the individual. Everyone has their own views on this. Personally I don't like to go on to the practice table just before the game. Some players always make a point of having ten minutes or so on the table beforehand. My feeling is that if you are building up to a major tournament you should already have put in sufficient practice.

If things are not going right during a match, again some players would get on the practice table during the interval to try and sort out the problems. I cannot see the benefit of this either, since for a start the conditions are totally different. The only way to learn is through experience of playing in front of large audiences, whether live or on television.

In some respects you need to approach a major tournament just as if you were playing in the club at home. I try to keep everything as normal as possible, just as though I was at an exhibition game. There is always the danger that you can get too hyped up for the occasion. I suffered from this when I went to defend my world title in 1986. You don't want to be too tensed up: equally, you shouldn't be too relaxed. You just have to find a happy medium which doesn't affect your natural game.

Joe Johnson is a good example of how to control your approach to big tournaments. He went to defend his world title in 1987 after having had a bad season and thinking he had little chance. He was very tensed up when he played Eugene Hughes in the first round, but having won on the last frame he then settled down and played his natural game. Remarkably it took him right through to the final again.

It's easy enough to tell someone who is just starting competitive snooker to forget about all the problems and missed shots and just to carry on with his natural game. He gets embarrassed and edgy about it and things go from bad to worse. It's one of the hardest things in the world, but you just have to stick with it.

That's where a good positive attitude helps so much, particularly when things aren't going as well as they could and you are trailing in a match. There have been plenty of times when I have been behind by two or three frames and you just have to say to yourself that if your opponent can win three or four frames then there is no reason why you can't do the same. When you're at the table, he just has to sit and watch you.

Aggression is also quite helpful, as long as you can control it. You have to make every tournament the one you must win. I have found that I play some of my best snooker when I get myself slightly angry inside. Obviously you musn't go over the top, or it will destroy your game. But really it's all to do with pride. Nobody wants to lose if they can help it – and certainly they don't want it to happen by playing badly.

Generally we all have good temperaments in the Matchroom. Obviously Steve and Terry are the most controlled. Jimmy and I are very similar in that after a match you probably couldn't tell whether we had won or lost. And Jimmy, of course, has this great knack of bouncing back immediately after a bad frame.

But these are not qualities that you can teach a snooker player. It's down to the individual and his personality. But I am sure the better the temperament, the better the player.

4 PLAYING SNOOKER

INTRODUCTION

This book has been carefully prepared by the Matchroom team to help you become a competent snooker player. The various sections have been structured in such a way as to provide a thorough introduction to the game by taking you, stage by stage, from the very basic techniques, through the more skilful aspects of ball and cue control to the fully advanced stages of speciality shots and competitive play.

We have all stressed the importance of mastering each technique from the beginning before moving on through the book, since learning to play the game successfully and consistently is a progressive exercise and one which you must take seriously and with full commitment if you want to achieve a reasonable standard of play.

Unfortunately the learning does not end there, for you need to work at your game regularly to maintain the progress you have hopefully made and ensure you do not adopt bad habits along the way.

In this section I have included a few final thoughts on how to sustain the effort and keep a check on your play, as well as some personal observations about the game and its players.

ANALYSING YOUR GAME

Playing a sport is all about enjoyment. But you still need to feel that you are playing it to the best of your ability to maintain that sense of fun, otherwise frustration can quickly step in and spoil it for you. This is why, even for the amateur who may only play once or twice a week, it is worth studying technique and trying to understand how this helps improve his game. For the better he can play, the more enjoyment he will get.

The hardest part about analysing technique and looking for ways to improve your overall game is when you are achieving some success through your own natural ability. One of the best examples of this is Terry, who as an amateur was playing tremendous snooker and met with immediate success when he turned professional. Then, suddenly, the standards within the professional game started to improve and Terry knew that there were aspects of his own game that he had to look at again.

It is a very brave thing to do at such a stage – to go back to the very basics of your technique and look for ways of improving them, particularly when you have been world champion! But he knew he wouldn't be satisfied in himself if he did not do this.

I remember when he turned professional that he would bridge with his hand flat on the table and stand with his feet together. He decided he must change these aspects of his technique to help him get better. He did – and success followed.

Terry has kept up with the general improvement in the game – and that in itself is a success story.

It is the easiest thing in the world to say: "Leave it alone. You will only cause confusion and upset what you already have." But Terry knew in himself that the only way to stay at the top was to keep checking on and working at his technique. This, I believe, is the perfect object lesson for any amateur who wants to better himself, whatever his standard.

IMPROVING YOUR GAME

Apart from working hard at your technique in practice, the best way to improve your game is by getting as close as you can to better players – and that means playing with them. It is amazing how much you can pick up and improve on through the example of others.

I found that having reached a certain level in the club I used to play in, there was nothing more I could learn from the players around me. So I started to travel round to find opposition that was better than myself. This is not to say that you have to leave your own club, but you should extend your horizons and look for stiffer competition.

Not only does this provide you with a more conducive atmosphere in which to improve your own play, but it gives you valuable contact with players of a higher standard from whom you can learn. And this is a vital aspect in the development of any keen amateur – both from the point of view of technique and temperament.

Part of this process inevitably involves copying, which is something every youngster wanting to learn the game does at some stage. This is not to say that you should copy other players just for the sake of it. But if you analyse those aspects of their play that you admire or feel they do particularly well, then this can prove very beneficial. Eventually you may also start to spot faults and weaknesses in a player you once thought a lot of.

The danger lies in copying something you don't really understand. I remember this happening with Alex Higgins, who used to tap his cue on the side of the table. Suddenly across the country, players would be tapping their cues, although they probably had no idea why they were doing it. The reason Alex did this was to get rid of excess chalk on his cue tip.

If you do feel inclined to copy anything from your favourite player, then watch the way he hits the ball.

DEDICATION

One of the problems when you are striving to develop your own game is the effect of having other much better players than yourself around all the time. This is where dedication and perserverance play such an important in any youngster's development. Neal is a very good example, in this respect.

He used to play at one of *the* clubs in London – the Ron Gross Snooker Centre. At that time there were some pretty good amateurs playing for the club – his father Geoff, Jimmy and Patsy Fagan. Refusing to be overawed by such illustrious company, Neal used to go away to one of the tables at the back of the club and practise hard. In modern day terms I suppose you would call him a late developer. But what he did was quietly get on with putting his game together. Then suddenly he was beating the best. No longer was he Geoff's son. Now Geoff is Neal's father.

I mention this to highlight how important it is to work hard at your game and be prepared to take the back seat for as long as it is necessary to master your game. There are always bound to be players better than yourself at most stages in your life, but you should never be overawed by this or let it upset your own game. Bide your time, get yourself ready and take the opportunity when it arises to show them how good a player you really are.

TEMPERAMENT

It has been mentioned before in the book, but I feel it cannot be stressed too strongly, that temperament plays a very important part in the success or failure on the table. Whether you are playing well or badly, self control is a great asset.

In this respect, think of snooker as a game of poker. Whatever may be going through your mind at the time, never let it show. Whatever advantage you may have conceded on the table, never give anything away to your opponent off it.

Even though Jimmy's nickname is The Whirlwind, in no way does this reflect his temperament when he's playing the game. In fact, he has one of the best attitudes to matchplay of any of the professionals. Whereas some players can get noticeably upset when things are going badly – and you can usually tell just by looking at them whether they are playing well or not – Jimmy is one of the hardest players to 'read'.

This is certainly a discipline you should concentrate on developing at every level of the game. Good control off the table means good control on it; the two go hand in hand. To control the balls you must first be in control of yourself.

SNOOKER SENSE

There is one particularly interesting quality in a snooker player that gives him that all-important edge over others of equal ability, which I call snooker sense – or intuition. It is not really something you can put your finger on and certainly nothing you can teach anyone. But it can make the difference

between winning and losing, remaining a top amateur or becoming a successful professional.

It's all about table cunning, being able to assess a shot in terms of safety or danger. It's the ability to sense whether a shot is too risky under the circumstances and to refrain from playing it where others would blindly strike out and come to grief. This situation occurs most commonly towards the end of a frame, where one mistake can prove fatal.

That's not to say that those who have this quality are more cautious as players. They know instinctively what are the big shots and seem to calculate the percentages more accurately. They always appear to choose the right time to press home the advantage when things are going well or close up the game when they are going badly.

The lesson to be learnt from such players is that you should not aim to be just an attacking or a defensive player – or a fast or slow player, for that matter. You must learn to play to the table, be ready to change up or down a gear, as necessary.

PRACTISING

Throughout this book we have included in the relevant sections ideas on practising the various techniques discussed. These should not only be helpful in mastering all those important aspects of the game but necessary to maintain specific skills. I find it enormously helpful to combine such exercises into a varied practice routine, which falls into three parts. I offer this as general guidance although you can of course set up your own.

Firstly I practise on my own, where I concentrate 100 per cent on technique, on moving the cue backwards and forwards and hitting the cue ball correctly.

Then I practise with my father, who is my coach, and together we put all those basics into play to make breaks. We are not playing seriously, but rather checking out the techniques, which I get my father to keep an eye on.

The third type of practice involves playing against a top local amateur and here I try to recreate as closely as possible a match situation. I hasten to add that no money is involved here! What we play for is the handicap I give the other player. This becomes a matter of pride to both of us.

We normally play the best of nine frames and each match is graded according to the result. If I win 5–4 or 5–3, for example, I give him one more point start next time – or take one away if I lose. If the result is 5–2 or 5–1, then two points are at stake. This way we are able to simulate matchplay conditions where you have to consider tactics as much as technique.

If playing for the pride of your handicap is not sufficient incentive, then you might want to consider playing for the table charges. Some people like playing for money, but I would issue a word of warning here. Never play for more than you can afford to lose. When we play in tournaments, we never actually lose money. We might not win as much, but we don't lose any of our own. I believe in a tournament you play for pride as much as money. So pride should be as much a thrill in practice, too.

GAMESMANSHIP

There is nowhere near the amount of gamesmanship in professional snooker as you might find in club snooker. At the top level you are concentrating so hard on playing well that you just haven't the time to worry about putting your opponent off.

There was a story I heard of an old player some years ago who would make suitable preparations before a match and at an appropriate moment in the game play a safety shot that brought the cue ball back to where he was standing. He would then pass wind. This of course left his opponent in a very uncomfortable, not to say volatile, position from which to take the next shot! That certainly required incredible body control!

In clubs I have seen players standing opposite their opponents as they prepare to play a shot or move just at the crucial moment. Chalking the cue is another tactic or muttering what a difficult shot the other person has got to play. But none of these are part of the professional game.

If you love the game enough and want to play it seriously, then you will never resort to this kind of behaviour. And if others do it to you, then you should not respond. If you can overcome such distractions and continue playing your normal game, this can only be to your advantage and you will improve your match temperament no end.

As professionals we do have to put up with a lot of distractions at times, such as people moving about in the audience, lighting a cigarette in your line of sight, rustling a crisp bag or coughing just as you are about to play the shot. Cameramen are only human and cannot be expected to stand like statues hour after hour. And occasionally the commentary box door is left open and you pick up someone's muffled voice. There is no point in making excuses about being put off. You have to learn to live with and play against these things.

At the end of the day, you must be able to respond in the best possible way – on the table.

THE MATCHROOM

A lot of people ask us how we get on together as a team when we have to play so much competitive snooker against each other. The answer is that while there is plenty of cammaraderie off the table, during exhibitions and when we are travelling abroad, when we are playing in a tournament we are all individuals and keep ourselves very much to ourselves.

On the whole we don't socialize together outside the snooker circuit, mainly because we all have our own family, friends and general interests. In this respect every player is different. The only thing we really have in common is our love for the game.

Within snooker all players generally mix well and there is very little animosity, despite the fact that obviously we all want to win and those players who are lower in the rankings are desperately trying to improve and reach the top. With the Matchroom players, we naturally get on better with each other because we are together more.

Interestingly, we tend not to discuss each other's game much and rarely offer advice when someone is off form. We will, of course, if we are asked – but only then if we feel qualified to talk about it. There are not many players in the game who analyse technique that closely and who are therefore in a position to give positive help.

Where we are all very lucky is in having Barry Hearn as our manager. To me, Barry is more than that – he is also a very close friend. But he is there to help all the Matchroom players – not on the table but with their business and, if necessary, personal affairs.

Barry is a great motivator because he understands people – and that's what managing is all about.

APPENDICES

Height: 6 ft 1½ in

Reach: Up to the blue spot

Cue: Ash one-piece originally, which I was given when I was 14; probably about 40 years old. I have had it cut near the splice and made into a two-piece.

Cue weight: 18¾ oz

Cue length: 4 ft 9¼ in

Cue value: £100

Extension: Threequarter-piece screw-on

Cue tip: Blue Diamond – 10 mm

Chalk: Green Triangle

Cue case: Standard aluminium, specially adapted

Case content: Knife, two files, glue, chalk, spare tips, special rest extension, Matchroom towel (my 'worry rag') and a bell with a Japanese inscription. It rings in the case, acting as a security alarm as well as a lucky charm!

Practice: I like to practise for up to two hours on my own, then with my father and finally play frames with a good player. For the week leading up to a tournament, I would spend half the time by myself and with my father and the other half playing frames. I dress casually.

Snooker books: I read all new books once, but my main reference is Joe Davis's *Complete Snooker*, which I check on when I'm working on new techniques.

Snooker heroes: Ray Reardon in his great days.

Started playing: When I was 14.

First club: Lee Green Working Man's Club, London

Greatest influence: My father

Best advice received: By Barry Hearn (but they are too numerous to remember) and Mick Binfield, an amateur, who once told me to stand squarer to the shot.

Longest session: I think it must have been 9½ hours playing for 2½p a point at the Leyton Midland Snooker Club. I also recall a marathon stint in the Lucania Championship some years ago when I played on and off between 10.30 am and 4 am the following morning!

Match preparation: I like to travel the night before if I'm playing an afternoon session. I try to eat up to four hours beforehand, which usually means a light breakfast! I will go on the practice table for 20–30 minutes and I allow about 15 minutes to get changed.

Relaxing during match: I will normally eat something after the afternoon session is finished, then watch TV. After that, it's back to the same routine.

Drink during match: Perrier, lemonade or water (if it tastes nice)

Best shot: It was against Ray Reardon during a match at Pontin's in Prestatyn. The pink was between the blue and brown spots with the white very close to the side cushion midway between the pink and black spots. I potted the pink into the bottom corner pocket and screwed the cue ball all the way back to get on the black.

Best match: My best win was my first World Championship in 1981. The best match, certainly for excitement, was the 1985 final against Dennis, which we'll all remember for a long, long time.

Favourite venue: The Guildhall, Preston, since it was where I had my first professional victory, the Coral UK Championship against Alex Higgins.

Favourite tournament: The World Championship

Favourite player: To watch, Ray Reardon and Alex Higgins at their peak – and Jimmy.

Favourite shot: Potting the pink into the top corner pocket and screwing back on to the far middle pocket jaw for position on the black – a clever finish if it doesn't matter.

Most important advice: Keep the head still on the shot.

Ambition: To play snooker well for as long as I can enjoy it.

Mascot: My Japanese bell and Matchroom 'worry rag'

Superstitions: No long-lasting ones, touch wood!

Nickname: Interesting, The Nugget and Golden Balls

Other interests: Collecting R & B and soul records, books, videos and watching sport generally – more than playing it (!) with the exception of a little cricket and golf

FACT FILE
NEAL FOULDS

Height: 6 ft 2 in

Reach: 3 in short of the blue spot

Cue: Maple two-piece, custom-made in 1985

Cue weight: 17 oz

Cue length: 4 ft 11 in

Cue value: £50–£60

Extension: None

Cue tip: Elkmaster – 8.5 mm; prefer using new tips.

Chalk: Green Triangle

Cue case: Specially made leather

Case content: I'm not a gadget person but I always keep some glue for emergency tip repairs

Practice: I aim to practise up to 4 hours every day. I don't practise much on my own, but usually try to play frames against a good opponent. I dress casually.

Snooker books: So far I've only ever read one – by John Spencer

Snooker heroes: Cliff Wilson, who used to have lots of battles with my father. He always seemed to enjoy the game so much

Started playing: When I was 11.

First club: The old snooker hall in Bond Street, Ealing

Greatest influence: My father and Ron Gross, who had a very good safety game

Best advice received: By Patsy Houlihan. He told me to stop wearing glasses and use contact lenses. The decision marked the biggest turning point in my game.

Longest session: I believe about 9 hours against Steve in the 1985 Embassy World Championship, when I lost 8–10.

Match preparation: Depending on the venue, my father drives me – normally the night before. I like to eat something light, such as a salad, and will give myself about 20 minutes on my own in the dressing room before the match.

Relaxing during match: If there was time I'd have a quick nap or watch TV in my hotel.

Drink during match: Perrier or orange juice

Best shot: A long screw-back during the 1986 BCE final against Cliff Thorburn. It was a long pot red with the cue ball about 6 in from the baulk cushion. I screwed back to get on the baulk colours and went on to make a 50 break, which put me within a frame of victory.

Best match: This was against Cliff Thorburn again, this time in the 1986 UK Championship, which I won 9–2. Although Cliff wasn't on top form, I played out of my skin.

Favourite venue: The Crucible, Sheffield. I love the atmosphere and the importance of the occasion.

Favourite tournament: The Rothmans International. I like The Hexagon in Reading, the tournament is always well supported and the players well looked after.

Favourite player: Ray Reardon in his heyday

Favourite shot: I enjoy long straight shots best.

Most important advice: Always practise seriously.

Ambition: To win the World Championship, of course, and more major tournaments.

Mascot: None

Superstitions: None – yet

Nickname: The press call me Busby, because I'm always on the phone. During my first tour of the Far East, the Matchroom boys called me Silence and so Steve suggested I bought a pair of squeaky shoes!

Other interests: My father and I own greyhounds. I also enjoy cricket, mainly watching.

FACT FILE
TERRY GRIFFITHS

Height: 5 ft 10 in

Reach: 6 in short of the blue spot

Cue: Maple one-piece, probably about 90 years old; hand-made and hand-spliced

Cue weight: 15 oz

Cue length: 4 ft 9 in

Cue value: £50

Extension: Slot-on

Cue tip: Elkmaster – 9.5 mm

Chalk: Blue National Tournament

Cue case: Aluminium

Case content: Knife, file, sandpaper, glue, tip shaper, special rest support, Matchroom towel, etc

Practice: As many hours as possible every day when I can. Of each hour, 55 minutes are enjoyment and the other five minutes hard work. I wear casual clothes.

Snooker books: I reckon I've read every book on snooker, especially Steve's – *Successful Snooker* – for the coaching side. And, of course, my own – *Complete Snooker*

Snooker heroes: Ray Reardon, who was the best in the game when I started playing.

Started playing: When I was 14.

First club: Hatchers in Llanelli

Greatest influence: My wife for her encouragement and support

Best advice received: By Mario Berni: "You'll never be successful until you've learnt to accept defeat." Nowhere was this more true than when I lost in the final of the Welsh Amateur Championship in 1972.

Longest session: Against Cliff Thorburn in the 1983 Embassy World Championship. It is still the latest finish in the history of the game, I believe. We started at 9 pm and finished at about 3.50 am.

Match preparation: I like to drive myself to matches and usually arrive the night before. I will not eat too soon beforehand and try to have an hour to myself.

Relaxing during match: I enjoy watching others play and like to practise as much as possible, even between sessions.

Drink during match: Water

Best shot: The black I potted to beat Steve in the final of the 1982 Lada Classic. That made it 9–8 after I had been 3–8 down and this was the first time Steve had been beaten in a televised tournament for 18 months. The cue ball was on the cushion and I had a three-quarter-ball black from its spot – a very difficult shot under pressure.

Best match: The 13–12 victory over Alex Higgins in the quarter-final of the 1979 World Championship, which of course I went on to win.

Favourite venue: The Guildhall, Preston

Favourite tournament: The World Championship

Favourite player: Steve, because he is the best

Favourite shot: The easy ones

Most important advice: To compete as much as possible in matchplay, since this is the best way to learn.

Ambition: To strike the cue ball perfectly every time.

Mascot: None

Superstitions: None at all

Nickname: Griff

Other interests: My family, golf, coaching, watching snooker and, of course, my own snooker club

Height: 5 ft 7 in

Reach: 9 in short of the blue spot

Cue: Ash one-piece, which I bought off a chap called Dave Pickles in Zan's Billiard Hall in Tooting, London, in 1976 and have trimmed slightly. I now have a second two-piece ash cue, hand-made, which was presented to me by the maker – Keith Auld of Wimbledon.

Cue weight: 17½ oz

Cue length: 4 ft 7 in

Cue value: Cost me £3 in 1976

Extension: Threequarter-piece screw-on for second cue

Cue tip: Elkmaster – 10 mm, which I cut down to 9.75 mm

Chalk: Green Triangle

Cue case: Standard aluminium

Case content: File, sandpaper, glue etc. Also a set of Chinese balls given to me by a friend from Hong Kong (see under Mascot).

Practice: I try to practise as much as possible, on average three hours a day, and more if possible before a tournament. I wear casual clothes.

Snooker books: I tend to look at sections and read bits here and there. I've looked at Terry's book.

Snooker heroes: John Spencer, whom I always regarded as a classy player with a lot of style. And the rest of the 'Big Three' in the earlier days – Ray Reardon and Alex Higgins.

Started playing: When I was 14.

First club: Zan's Billiard Club, Tooting, London

Greatest influence: Barry Hearn, who has helped me so much commercially since I turned professional, and two good friends who previously managed me – Bob Davis and Henry West.

Best advice received: By my mother, who said: "Never forget who you are or where you've come from – whatever happens."

Longest session: I remember years ago playing 24 hours non-stop on 'points' at Zan's. And I've had a few long games with Cliff Thorburn, of course.

Match preparation: Depending on the venue I prefer to travel the night before. I will have a light snack a few hours before the match and do things to take my mind off the game, such as walking and watching TV.

Relaxing during match: During the short breaks, I'll sit in the dressing room and probably read. Between sessions I'd eat straight away and then relax and watch TV in my hotel.

Drink during match: Mineral water

Best shot: Difficult – there have been so many!

Best match: Definitely my first victory against Steve in the semi-final of the 1986 Tolly Cobbold English Championship, which I went on to win 9–7 against Neal. Otherwise I would think the 1984 Lada Classic when I lost to 'You Know Who' 8–9.

Favourite venue: Wembley Conference Centre and The Crucible, Sheffield

Favourite tournament: The UK and World Championships, because they are longer and I think fairer.

Favourite player: Really I have no favourites, since I admire different qualities in many players. Jimmy and I are great buddies, then there's Steve and Terry – and Alex Higgins when he's buzzing . . .

Favourite shot: The match-winning one, particularly when you get it first time. It may not be the most difficult, but it's certainly the most important.

Most important advice: Practise as hard as you can. You have to give up a lot of things to reach the top, so be prepared to make sacrifices.

Ambition: To be world champion and to be Number One, which isn't so easy!

Mascot: My Chinese balls which an actor and rock musician friend David Cheung gave me in Hong Kong. He also makes 100 breaks! I also take into tournaments things that people send me. In 1986 and 1987 at Ipswich I had a lucky penguin.

Superstitions: Nothing serious, but if I walk through one door and then win the match, the chances are I'll walk through the same door next time.

Nickname: Disco Kid when I was younger; also Tornado

Other interests: Horse racing, music, cricket, table tennis

FACT FILE

DENNIS TAYLOR

Height: 5 ft 9 in

Reach: 6 in short of the blue spot

Cue: Maple two-piece, about 10 years old; originally a threequarter cue made many years ago, with middle section cut out; slightly thicker butt end.

Cue weight: 17½ oz

Cue length: 4 ft 9 in

Cue value: £50–£90

Extension: Slot-on

Cue tip: Blue Diamond – 10 mm; use new tips all the time.

Chalk: Green Triangle

Cue case: Specially made to take my specs!

Case content: Scalpel, file, sandpaper, glue and general gadgetry

Practice: I aim to practise up to 1½ hours per day on average, normally playing from the break off against myself. I wear casual clothes, although when an amateur I used to dress up.

Snooker books: I've never read a tactical book – until now!

Snooker heroes: John Spencer, against whom I used to play exhibition matches. He was responsible for getting me accepted as a professional.

Started playing: When I was 9.

First club: Jim Joe's in Coalisland, Northern Ireland

Greatest influence: My mother and an elderly woman I called Granny, who used to give me sixpences when I was a boy so I could go and practise. More recently my wife, who has had a lot to put up with.

Best advice received: By Joe Davis, who once told me: "You are never going to become a better potter. The way you are going to improve is to eliminate shots from your game."

Longest session: As an amateur at the old Post Office Club in Blackburn – from 1 pm until 11 pm. As a professional against Steve in the 1985 Embassy World Championship final session – from 7 pm until 12.40 am.

Match preparation: I used to drive myself to venues to arrive at least two hours before the start. I never eat within two hours of playing. Otherwise no special preparation.

Relaxing during match: Between sessions I watch TV in my hotel. Otherwise no special routine.

Drink during match: Perrier or iced water.

Best shot: Against Fred Davis in the 1975 Pot Black competition. Fred needed a snooker on the pink and left me with the pink touching the cushion on the baulk line and the cue ball on the same cushion near the top of the table. I potted the pink and screwed back a long way to get on the black.

Best match: This has to be the 1985 Embassy World Championship final against Steve, when I came back to win after trailing 8–0. Others include my victory against Cliff Thorburn in the 1984 Rothmans International and the 1987 Benson & Hedges Masters final, when I beat Alex Higgins 9–8 after trailing 5–8.

Favourite venue: Hexagon, Reading, followed by The Crucible, Sheffield.

Favourite tournament: Embassy World Championship, followed by the Rothmans International.

Favourite player: I particularly enjoy watching Jimmy White.

Favourite shot: A long pot the full length of the table, screwing the cue ball right back. You need tremendous accuracy for this.

Most important advice: Keep your head still and deliver the cue in a straight line.

Ambition: Naturally to win the World Championship again, but most importantly to continue enjoying snooker.

Mascot: None

Superstitions: None

Nickname: None that I'm aware of!

Other interests: Golf, watching TV and, of course, the family

FACT FILE

WILLIE THORNE

Height: 6 ft 2 in

Reach: Up to the blue spot

Cue: Maple one-piece which my mother bought new for me when I was 14; the butt end has been patched up several times. I also have a second, two-piece cue.

Cue weight: 17½ oz

Cue length: 4 ft 10 in

Cue value: It cost my mother £3 2s 6d.

Extension: I don't use one with my one-piece cue. I have a screw-on extension for my two-piece.

Cue tip: Elkmaster – 10 mm. I always use second-hand tips.

Chalk: Green Triangle

Cue case: Hand-made leather from a saddler in Cornwall. It was a present from David Taylor and must be worth over £400.

Case content: Emergency kit including second-hand tips, file, sandpaper, glue, extra chalk, etc.

Practice: Usually in the mornings and up to 3 hours per day before a tournament – at least five days for general matches and up to a month before major tournaments. I dress very casually.

Snooker books: I've never read a snooker book.

Snooker heroes: John Spencer, Ray Reardon, John Pullman and Fred Davis

Started playing: When I was 14 at the Anstey Conservative Club.

First club: North Evington Working Man's Club in Leicestershire

Greatest influence: My parents and Brian Cakebread, coach at Osborne's in Leicester

Best advice received: By Brian Cakebread: "Head down and follow through".

Longest session: I believe against Cliff Thorburn – about four hours.

Match preparation: I like to travel the night before, depending on the venue, and get a good night's sleep. I practise for an hour at the venue when possible, change about half-an-hour before the match and relax. I don't like being alone.

Relaxing during match: I will practise if I'm playing badly; otherwise I will probably watch TV and maybe go out for a meal.

Drink during match: Lucozade

Best shot: In the semi-final of the 1985 Mercantile Credit Classic against Steve. We were level on frames at 8–8. I went to pot a red on the edge of the pack with the cue ball on the jaws of the middle pocket. I potted the red and kept position on the blue. I went on to make a 60 break, won the match and then the tournament.

Best match: The final of the 1986 UK Championship – until the last session!

Favourite venue: Birchwood Centre, Warrington, and The Crucible, Sheffield

Favourite tournament: The World and UK Championships because they are the right length for the best players.

Favourite player: Jimmy and Stephen Hendry. They play snooker the way it should be played, knocking balls in as quickly as possible. This makes the game much more exciting.

Favourite shot: The last black when I'm on 140 that's impossible to miss – and screwing back specific distances.

Most important advice: Make sure you've got the natural ability and practise every day. If you don't have the natural ability, don't expect miracles.

Ambition: To win the World Championship.

Mascot: None

Superstitions: Just walking under ladders

Nickname: The Great WT and Gonzo

Other interests: Football, golf and horseracing

FACT FILE

JIMMY WHITE

Height: 5 ft 10 in

Reach: 3 in short of the blue spot

Cue: Ash two-piece, five years old; having broken previous cue, bought present one just a week before my first success in a professional ranking tournament.

Cue weight: 19 oz

Cue length: 4 ft 10 in

Cue value: £100

Extension: Screw-on

Cue tip: Elkmaster – 9.25 mm; like to play with them broken in.

Chalk: Green Triangle

Cue case: Wooden

Case content: Knife, file, sandpaper, glue and two lucky charms (see under Mascot)

Practice: I try to practise three hours every day. Usually this involves knocking the balls around. I have no special routine. I always dress casually.

Snooker books: I've looked at a few, but mainly *Spencer on Snooker.*

Snooker heroes: I was a great Alex Higgins fan when I was younger; also John Spencer and Ray Reardon.

Started playing: When I was 11.

First club: Zan's Billiard Club, Tooting, London

Greatest influence: My father, for his inspiration and encouragement

Best advice received: From Ronnie Gross, who gave me a lot of general advice on how to improve my game and attitude. It worked within weeks.

Longest session: In professional tournaments my matches tend not to last too long. The longest I played was at Zan's when I was 15. That was for two days, when I was playing for £1 a frame. I came out tired but with a full pocket!

Match preparation: I try to get into the best possible frame of mind and make sure I'm ready about an hour before. I like to have about 15 minutes on the table beforehand. I'll eat a light lunch and have my main meal afterwards.

Relaxing during match: When there's time, I enjoy playing a bit of golf or going to the cinema. In between sessions I'll relax in my hotel and probably watch some television.

Drink during match: Water

Best shot: In the 1988 Benson & Hedges when Doug Mountjoy snookered me on the pink. I used screw and side to come off the cushion and potted the pink to clinch the frame.

Best match: Ironically the two I remember best were matches I lost. They were the 1987 Tennants UK Championship against Steve and back in 1982 when I went out to Alex Higgins in the Embassy World Championships.

Favourite venue: The Wembley Conference Centre, London

Favourite tournament: The World Championship

Favourite shot: None in particular. I just enjoy playing the whole game.

Most important advice: Absorb all the experience you can and don't get too disappointed when you lose.

Ambition: To be Number One and win the World Championship.

Mascot: I have two I carry around in my cue case. One is a good luck charm with my name on that I was given by a friend in Hong Kong and the other is an old snuff box that was given to me by an old boy in a working man's club in London once.

Superstitions: None

Nickname: Snowy, The Whirlwind

Other interests: Golf, family and horseracing

CAREER RECORD

STEVE DAVIS

1980 Coral UK Championship v Alex Higgins – won 16-6

1981 Yamaha International Masters v David Taylor – won 9-6
John Courage English Championship v Tony Meo – won 9-3
Embassy World Championship v Doug Mountjoy – won 18-12
Jameson International v Dennis Taylor – won 9-0
Coral UK Championship v Terry Griffiths – won 16-3
Northern Ireland Classic v Jimmy White – lost 9-11

1982 Lada Classic v Terry Griffiths – lost 8-9
Benson & Hedges Masters v Terry Griffiths – won 9-5
Yamaha International Masters v Terry Griffiths – won 9-7
Tolly Cobbold Classic v Dennis Taylor – won 8-3
Benson & Hedges Irish Masters v Terry Griffiths – lost 5-9
Langs Scottish Masters v Alex Higgins – won 9-4

1983 Lada Classic v Bill Werbeniuk – won 9-5
Tolly Cobbold Classic v Terry Griffiths – won 8-5
Benson & Hedges Irish Masters v Ray Reardon – won 9-2
Embassy World Championship v Cliff Thorburn – won 18-6
Langs Scottish Masters v Tony Knowles – won 9-6
Jameson International v Cliff Thorburn – won 9-4
Coral UK Championship v Alex Higgins – lost 15-16

1984 Lada Classic v Tony Meo – won 9-8
Benson & Hedges Irish Masters v Terry Griffiths – won 9-1

Tolly Cobbold Classic v Tony Knowles – won 8-2
Embassy World Championship v Jimmy White – won 18-16
Langs Supreme Scottish Masters v Jimmy White – won 9-4
Jameson International v Tony Knowles – won 9-2
Coral UK Open v Alex Higgins – won 16-8

1985 Tolly Cobbold English Championship v Tony Knowles – won 9-2
Embassy World Championship v Dennis Taylor – lost 17-18
Rothmans Grand Prix v Dennis Taylor – won 10-9
Coral UK Open v Willie Thorne – won 16-14
Kit Kat v Dennis Taylor – lost 5-9

1986 Dulux British Open v Willie Thorne – won 12-7
Embassy World Championship v Joe Johnson – lost 12-18
BCE Canadian Masters v Willie Thorne – won 9-3
Tennants UK Championship v Neal Foulds – won 16-7
Mercantile Credit Classic v Jimmy White – won 13-12
Benson & Hedges Irish Masters v Willie Thorne – won 9-1

1987 Embassy World Championship v Joe Johnson – won 18-14
Fidelity Unit Trust International v Cliff Thorburn – won 12-5
Tennants UK Championship v Jimmy White – won 16-14

1988 Mercantile Credit Classic v John Parrott – won 13-11
Benson & Hedges Masters v Mike Hallett – won 9-0

163

NEAL FOULDS

1986 Tolly Cobbold English Championship v Tony Meo – lost 7-9
BCE International v Cliff Thorburn – won 12-9
Tennants UK Championship v Steve Davis – lost 7-16

1987 Dulux British Open v Jimmy White – lost 9-13

1988 Tolly Cobbold English Championship v Dean Reynolds – lost 5-9

TERRY GRIFFITHS

1979 Embassy World Championship v Dennis Taylor – won 24-16
Coral UK Championship v John Virgo – lost 13-14

1980 Benson & Hedges Masters v Alex Higgins – won 9-5
Benson & Hedges Irish Masters v Doug Mountjoy – won 9-8

1981 Benson & Hedges Masters v Alex Higgins – lost 6-9
Coral UK Championship v Steve Davis – lost 3-16

1982 Lada Classic v Steve Davis – won 9-8
Benson & Hedges Masters v Steve Davis – lost 5-9
Yamaha International Masters v Steve Davis – lost 7-9
Woodpecker Welsh Championship v Doug Mountjoy – lost 8-9
Benson & Hedges Irish Masters v Steve Davis – won 9-5
Coral UK Championship v Alex Higgins – won 16-15

1983 Tolly Cobbold Classic v Steve Davis – lost 5-7

1984 Benson & Hedges Masters v Jimmy White – lost 5-9
Benson & Hedges Irish Masters v Steve Davis – lost 1-9

1985 BCE Welsh Championship v Doug Mountjoy – won 9-4

1986 BCE Belgian Classic v Kirk Stevens – won 9-7
Zetters Welsh Championship v Doug Mountjoy – won 9-3

TONY MEO

1981 John Courage English Championship v Steve Davis – lost 3-9

1984 Lada Classic v Steve Davis – lost 8-9

1985 Winfield Australian Masters v John Campbell – won 7-2

1986 Tolly Cobbold English Championship v Neal Foulds – won 9-7

1987 Tolly Cobbold English Championship v Les Dodd – won 9-5

DENNIS TAYLOR

1979 Embassy World Championship v Terry Griffiths – lost 16-24

1981 Jameson International v Steve Davis – lost 0-9

1982 Tolly Cobbold Classic v Steve Davis – lost 3-8
      Irish Championship v Alex Higgins – won 16-13

1983 Irish Championship v Alex Higgins – lost 11-16

1984 Rothmans Grand Prix v Cliff Thorburn – won 10-2

1985 Irish Championship v Alex Higgins – won 10-5
      Embassy World Championship v Steve Davis – won 18-17
      Rothmans Grand Prix v Steve Davis – lost 9-10
      BCE Canadian Masters v Steve Davis – won 9-5
      Kit Kat v Steve Davis – won 9-5

1986 Strongbow Irish Championship v Alex Higgins – won 10-7

1987 Benson & Hedges Masters v Alex Higgins – won 9-8
      Rothmans Grand Prix v Stephen Hendry – lost 7-10
      Matchroom Irish Professional Championship v J O'Boye –
      won 5-2

WILLIE THORNE

1985 Mercantile Credit Classic v Cliff Thorburn – won 13-8
Langs Scottish Masters v Cliff Thorburn – lost 7-9
Coral UK Open v Steve Davis – lost 14-16

1986 Dulux British Open v Steve Davis – lost 7-12
Benson & Hedges Irish Masters v Jimmy White – lost 5-9

JIMMY WHITE

1981 Langs Supreme Scottish Masters v Cliff Thorburn – won 9-4
Northern Ireland Classic v Steve Davis – won 11-9

1982 Professional Players Tournament v Ray Reardon – lost 5-10

1983 Yamaha International Masters v Ray Reardon – lost 6-9

1984 Benson & Hedges Masters v Terry Griffiths – won 9-5
Embassy World Championship v Steve Davis – lost 16-18
Langs Supreme Scottish Masters v Steve Davis – lost 4-9
Carlsberg Challenge v Tony Knowles – won 9-7

1985 Benson & Hedges Irish Masters v Alex Higgins – won 9-5
Carlsberg Challenge v Alex Higgins – won 8-3
Goya Matchroom Trophy v Cliff Thorburn – lost 10-12

1986 Mercantile Credit Classic v Cliff Thorburn – won 13-12
Benson & Hedges Masters v Cliff Thorburn – lost 5-9
Benson & Hedges Irish Masters v Willie Thorne – won 9-5

1987 Dulux British Open v Neal Foulds – won 13-9
Tennants UK Championship v Steve Davis – lost 14-16